DISCARD

JESSE JAMES

THE CHELSEA HOUSE LIBRARY OF BIOGRAPHY

JESSE JAMES

T. J. STILES

Chelsea House Publishers

New York · Philadelphia

CHELSEA HOUSE PUBLISHERS

Editorial Director   Richard Rennert
Executive Managing Editor   Karyn Gullen Browne
Executive Editor   Sean Dolan
Copy Chief   Robin James
Picture Editor   Adrian G. Allen
Art Director   Robert Mitchell
Manufacturing Director   Gerald Levine
Systems Manager   Lindsey Ottman
Production Coordinator   Marie Claire Cebrián-Ume

The Chelsea House Library of Biography
Senior Editor   Kathy Kuhtz

Staff for **JESSE JAMES**
Associate Editor   Martin Schwabacher
Editorial Assistant   Mary B. Sisson
Picture Researcher   Sandy Jones
Designer   Basia Niemczyc
Cover Illustration   Daniel O'Leary

3   5   7   9   8   6   4

Library of Congress Cataloging-in-Publication Data

Stiles, T. J.
Jesse James / T. J. Stiles.
p. cm.—(The Chelsea House library of biography)
Includes bibliographical references and index.
Summary: A biography of the outlaw, focusing on his involvement in the Civil
War and the formation of the James Gang.
ISBN 0-7910-1737-0
      0-7910-1738-9 (pbk.)
1. James, Jesse, 1847–1882—Juvenile literature. 2. Outlaws—West (U.S.)—
Biography—Juvenile literature. 3. Missouri—History—Civil War, 1861–
1865—Juvenile literature. 4. Kansas—History—Civil War, 1861–1865
—Juvenile literature. 5. Frontier and pioneer life—West (U.S.)—Juvenile literature.
6. West (U.S.)—History—Civil War, 1861–1865—Underground move-
ments—Juvenile literature. [1. James, Jesse, 1847–1882. 2. Robbers and out-
laws. 3. Frontier and pioneer life—West (U.S.) 4. West (U.S.)—History.   5.
United States—History—Civil War, 1861–1865—Underground movements.]
I. Title. II. Series.
F594.J27S75 1994   92-45210
346.1'552'092—dc20   CIP
[B]   AC

Contents

THE CHELSEA HOUSE LIBRARY OF BIOGRAPHY

Other titles in the series are forthcoming.

Introduction

Learning from Biographies

Vito Perrone

The oldest narratives that exist are biographical. Much of what we know, for example, about the Pharaohs of ancient Egypt, the builders of Babylon, the philosophers of Greece, the rulers of Rome, the many biblical and religious leaders who provide the base for contemporary spiritual beliefs, has come to us through biographies—the stories of their lives. Although an oral tradition was long the mainstay of historically important biographical accounts, the oral stories making up this tradition became by the 1st century A.D. central elements of a growing written literature.

In the 1st century A.D., biography assumed a more formal quality through the work of such writers as Plutarch, who left us more than 500 biographies of political and intellectual leaders of Rome and Greece. This tradition of focusing on great personages lasted well into the 20th century and is seen as an important means of understanding the history of various times and places. We learn much, for example, from Plutarch's writing about the collapse of the Greek city-states and about the struggles in Rome over the justice and the constitutionality of a world empire. We also gain considerable understanding of the definitions of morality and civic virtue and how various common men and women lived out their daily existence.

Not surprisingly, the earliest American writing, beginning in the 17th century, was heavily biographical. Those Europeans who came to America were dedicated to recording their experience, especially the struggles they faced in building what they determined to be a new culture. John Norton's *Life and Death of John Cotton*, printed in 1630, typifies these early works. Later biographers often tackled more ambitious projects. Cotton Mather's *Magnalia Christi Americana*, published in 1702, accounted for the lives of more than 70 ministers and political leaders. In addition, a biographical literature around the theme of Indian captivity had considerable popularity. Soon after the American Revolution and the organization of the United States of America, Americans were treated to a large outpouring of biographies about such figures as Benjamin Franklin, George Washington, Thomas Jefferson, and Aaron Burr, among others. These particular works served to build a strong sense of national identity.

Among the diverse forms of historical literature, biographies have been over many centuries the most popular. And in recent years interest in biography has grown even greater, as biography has gone beyond prominent government figures, military leaders, giants of business, industry, literature, and the arts. Today we are treated increasingly to biographies of more common people who have inspired others by their particular acts of courage, by their positions on important social and political issues, or by their dedicated lives as teachers, town physicians, mothers, and fathers. Through this broader biographical literature, much of which is featured in the CHELSEA HOUSE LIBRARY OF BIOGRAPHY, our historical understandings can be enriched greatly.

What makes biography so compelling? Most important, biography is a human story. In this regard, it makes of history something personal, a narrative with which we can make an intimate connection. Biographers typically ask us as readers to accompany them on a journey through the life of another person, to see some part of the world through another's eyes. We can, as a result, come to understand what it is like to live the life of a slave, a farmer, a textile worker, an engineer, a poet, a president—in a sense, to walk in another's shoes. Such experience can be personally invaluable. We cannot ask for a better entry into historical studies.

Although our personal lives are likely not as full as those we are reading about, there will be in most biographical accounts many common experiences. As with the principal character of any biography, we are also faced with numerous decisions, large and small. In the midst of living our lives we are not usually able to comprehend easily the significance of our daily decisions or grasp easily their many possible consequences, but we can gain important insights into them by seeing the decisions made by others play themselves out. We can learn from others.

Because biography is a personal story, it is almost always full of surprises. So often, the personal lives of individuals we come across historically are out of view, their public personas masking who they are. It is through biography that we gain access to their private lives, to the acts that define who they are and what they truly care about. We see their struggles within the possibilities and limitations of life, gaining insight into their beliefs, the ways they survived hardships, what motivated them, and what discouraged them. In the process we can come to understand better our own struggles.

As you read this biography, try to place yourself within the subject's world. See the events as that person sees them. Try to understand why the individual made particular decisions and not others. Ask yourself if you would have chosen differently. What are the values or beliefs that guide the subject's actions? How are those values or beliefs similar to yours? How are they different from yours? Above all, remember: You are engaging in an important historical inquiry as you read a biography, but you are also reading a literature that raises important personal questions for you to consider.

Jesse Woodson James led a notorious gang of outlaws in more than a dozen bank and train robberies between 1866 and 1882.

1

The Defeat of
the James Gang

EARLY IN THE MONTH OF SEPTEMBER 1876, eight men mounted on unusually powerful horses galloped across the Iowa border into Minnesota. They rode with an ease that stemmed from years on horseback, and they wore long linen coats known as dusters, the kind cattlemen wore when they drove their herds. The dusters kept off the grime kicked up during a long ride—and they were perfect for hiding guns. Each man carried two, four, or even six revolvers under his coat, with plenty of extra ammunition, and they handled their pistols as easily as their mounts. They were counting on theses talents for the days ahead.

The riders had come far from their homes in Missouri, but even here on the Minnesota border they were well known as the most dangerous outlaws in America. The three who led the group, in particular, had become household names. One was Frank James, a lanky man in his early thirties, with a neat mustache under a long nose. Another was Cole Younger, a huge man with a drooping mustache, heavy sideburns, and bulging eyes. His brothers Bob and Jim rode with the gang as it

11

traveled north. The last of the trio had won the greatest
fame of all, emerging as a legend in his own time. A few
years younger than his brother Frank, this tall, powerful
man watched the road with sharp blue eyes that blinked
constantly over his heavy black beard. His name was Jesse
James.

In addition to the James and Younger brothers, three
other men rode with the band as it made its way across the
southern Minnesota Plain. William Stiles (also known as
Bill Chadwell), the only clean-shaven man in the group,
guided the band as it crossed the Iowa state line. Stiles had
lived in Minnesota before joining the bandits, and he
promised them a land of rich banks that they could rob at
will. Clell Miller and Samuel Wells (also known as Charlie
Pitts), two men from near the western Missouri homes of
the James and Younger families, filled out the gang.

Jesse James was not yet 29, but he had already become
the most wanted man in Missouri, if not the entire United
States. He had started his career with the horse and revolver at the age of 16, when he ran off to join the Confederate bushwhackers during the Civil War. He took part in
the bitter guerrilla struggle against the Union army in Missouri during the war, learning to ambush (or "bushwhack")
and kill before he could even grow a beard. His older
brother Frank had fought as a guerrilla as well, serving
under Cole Younger for a time. After the war, Jesse had
risen to lead a gang that for almost 10 years had pulled off
spectacular bank and train robberies and escaped countless
hunts by local posses, the St. Louis police, and the re-
nowned Pinkerton detectives from Chicago.

No one, it seemed, could touch him. The farmers and
townspeople of western Missouri saw Jesse James as a
hero like Robin Hood who robbed the rich and gave to the
poor. The executives of the banks and railroad companies
he chose as targets thought of him as a ruthless bandit and
a cold-blooded murderer. Politicians argued about why he
went free year after year while Missouri became notorious

THE JAMES GANG'S ROBBERIES

as "the robber state." Many people who knew where Jesse James lived and what he looked like feared his revolvers too much to help arrest him. His mother, of course, considered him a brave boy and a good son who had suffered unjustly at the hands of the state authorities. One way or another, everyone had an opinion about Jesse James.

Despite all the attention, Jesse James continued to strike when and where he pleased, usually in the company of Frank and the Younger brothers. The police and county sheriffs still had no reliable description or photographs of the outlaws. On this particular September day the gang rode into Mankato, a prosperous town on the banks of the Minnesota River. But they were unusually cautious as they made their way through the Mankato streets. They were far from the land they knew so well, the woods and farmland of Missouri where they had been raised. Here, far to the north, they had to rely on the judgment of Bill Stiles, a man who had been with the gang only a short time.

The gang kept only the loosest organization, and its membership often changed from one robbery to the next, partly because several months usually passed between raids. Clell Miller lived near the James family in Clay County, Missouri, and he had taken part in many of the bank and train holdups. Bob and Jim Younger, too, were regular members of the gang, as was their brother John Younger before the Pinkerton detectives killed him one day on a Missouri country road. Other friends and relatives of the two families had helped out on earlier robberies as well.

But since the end of the 1860s, not long after the gang first came together in 1866, the leaders had remained Cole Younger, Frank, and especially Jesse James. They had fought together as Confederate guerrillas, learning their trade well enough to survive a war that took the lives of some of the deadliest killers in the West. Now they had emerged as the most successful bandits in the country. No matter how the gang changed from job to job, these three always kept things running smoothly.

But here in Minnesota they seemed to sense that they traveled in a more dangerous environment. Always in the past they had robbed banks and trains near their homes in Missouri, in territory they had ridden through since before the Civil War. They had once raided a northern state, Iowa, but they had stayed within an easy ride back to Missouri. Now they were delving deep into strange territory, led by a man who was not a part of their brotherhood of former Confederate guerrillas. So they cautiously scouted out the town and countryside, pretending to be stock buyers who had come to purchase cattle. With their fine horses and long linen dusters they looked the part. When they decided to rob the Mankato bank, a crowd on the street made them think they had been detected, and they quickly rode out of town. Stiles said he knew of another bank in the town of Northfield, not far east of Mankato.

Northfield seemed like the perfect target. The sleepy home to Scandinavian farmers and the private colleges of Carleton and St. Olaf, it sat on the eastern bank of the Cannon River about 40 miles south of St. Paul. On September 7, 1876, the gang gathered on the far side of the Cannon and made plans to rob the First National Bank. Leaving three men just west of the river, five of the bandits rode across the bridge into town with all the confidence of men who had robbed many banks before.

The five rode across the town's main square and dismounted in front of the First National Bank. Two men waited outside, revolvers ready under their linen dusters, as the other three went inside. Two men worked in the bank that day, Joseph Heywood and A. E. Bunker. Heywood, a substitute for the regular cashier, stepped up to help the three strangers. Instead, he found himself staring at three pistols. The bandits jumped over the counter and ordered Heywood to open the safe, but he refused. As one of them pressed a knife against the cashier's throat, Bunker broke and ran from the building.

In 10 years of armed robbery, nothing like this had ever happened to Jesse James. As long as Heywood

The town of Northfield, Minnesota, as it appeared around 1900. Jesse James and his gang ventured far from their home turf in Missouri when they attempted to rob the First National Bank (center) in Northfield in 1876.

resisted, the outlaws could do nothing. Meanwhile, Bunker screamed for help as he dashed for the street. One of the bandits fired at Bunker as he ran, putting a bullet in his shoulder. When Heywood continued to refuse to open the safe, the other outlaw slit his throat, then shot him in the head. Finding the cash drawers almost empty, the three leapt back over the counter and ran outside.

They burst straight into a gunfight. The two men standing guard outside had already attracted attention by stopping people from entering the bank. Then Bunker's shouts alerted the town to what was happening, and the men of Northfield ran to get their guns. Two businessmen from across the street, A. B. Manning and Henry Wheeler, loaded their rifles and began firing at the lookouts from their windows. A medical student home visiting his family took a gun and began shooting from a hotel room. The bandits fired back as they remounted, screaming at the people in the street to clear out of the way. One man, a Swede named Nicholas Gustavson, did not understand English and made no response to the outlaws' orders. They shot him dead for his ignorance.

The three men on the edge of town rode across the bridge when they heard the firing, and lead started snapping above their heads as well. The local men shot with deadly accuracy, firing from protected positions inside the buildings on the square. Clell Miller fell dead. Then Bill

Stiles—the man they needed to lead them through the Minnesota countryside—collapsed to the ground with a bullet in his chest. As the outlaws finally started to ride out of town, one of the townsmen shot down Bob Younger's horse, and then Bob himself fell under the impact of a rifle bullet. Cole galloped back under a storm of rifle fire and pulled his brother up behind him. The bodies of Miller and Stiles lay in the street as the gang raced away.

As the shattered gang galloped south, the Northfield telegraph operator sent word of the raid throughout the state. Scores of local residents joined posses to look for the bandits. One of these groups caught up with them and opened fire, killing Samuel Wells and badly wounding some of the other survivors. The gang made a narrow escape, but the pursuit grew even hotter.

With William Stiles dead, the outlaws simply rode south toward Missouri. But Bob Younger suffered so badly from his wounds that he could not bear the horse's bouncing trot.

This photograph of the town square in Northfield, Minnesota, taken a few years before the James gang's attempted robbery, shows the bridge the bandits crossed as they approached the town square. The bank where the robbery took place can be seen at center right (the building with arches).

Jesse James, already distressed by the disastrous raid, flew into a rage. He told Cole Younger that they had to either kill Bob or leave him behind. Cole refused, and the two shouted at each other as the hunting parties of Minnesotans drew closer. Finally Jesse and Frank broke away from the Younger brothers and rode off on their own. As Cole led his brothers south, Jesse decided to turn west instead.

The decision saved the James boys' lives and their freedom. The split confused the posses, who continued to look for a single group. As the brothers rode west across the state, toward South Dakota, the Minnesota lawmen converged on the badly wounded Youngers as they moved south. Eventually Cole and his brothers—exhausted by the chase and surrounded by armed Minnesotans—surrendered to their pursuers. The three brothers recovered from their injuries, stood trial, and went to prison with life sentences for their role in the Northfield robbery.

Of the eight men who had ridden into Minnesota only a few days before, only Jesse and Frank James remained alive and free. Bleeding from gunshot wounds and short on food and supplies, they had ridden through four states, eluding every detective, sheriff, and posse between St. Paul and Kansas City, until they finally made it back to the safety of their friends and relatives in western Missouri. Their wounds would eventually heal, and they would even go on to ride and rob again. But never before had the gang been so clearly defeated as on that summer day in Northfield. The James-Younger gang, the terror of every bank and railroad west of the Mississippi, vanished in the quiet farmland of southern Minnesota.

Opposite:
A montage of photographs shows the key players in the Northfield raid. Counter-clockwise from the far left are captured gang members Cole Younger, Jim Younger, Charlie Pitts, Bob Younger, and (center) William Stiles (also known as Bill Chadwell) and Clell Miller. Stiles, Miller, and Pitts were all killed in the fighting; Bob and Jim Younger were seriously wounded. Clockwise from upper left are Northfield citizens August Suborn, Joseph Heywood (the cashier killed for refusing to open the safe), and Sheriff Glispin.

Jesse James spent his childhood in the border region between Missouri and Kansas. The atmosphere of violence and intimidation created by the continuing struggle between proslavery and antislavery forces on the Border had a lasting effect on his character.

2

Child of the Border

IN 1842, A YOUNG BAPTIST PREACHER named Robert James and his wife, Zerelda, left their home in Lexington, Kentucky, to visit Robert's mother-in-law in northwestern Missouri. No railroads ran across Missouri in those years, just dirt tracks for horses and coaches, so the newlyweds probably took the most common route to the western border, traveling by boat up the broad Missouri River. From St. Louis—a growing city bustling with new workshops, stores, cattle yards, and immigrants from Europe—the river wound through plantation country in the center of the state, where slaves harvested thousands of acres of hemp and tobacco. Farther west, the river took them to the western frontier, a region of woods, brush, and corn and hog farms; few of the towns contained more than a church and a few stores. Here, in the part of the state known as the Border, because it was then the boundary between the organized states and Indian lands, the newlywed couple decided to stay and raise a family.

In this autographed photo the young Jesse James looks more like the Baptist minister's son that he was than the hardened killer he would become.

The Border would shape the lives of Jesse James and his family, and it was a land unlike any other part of the country. On this raw, sometimes violent frontier all the different sections of the United States came together—slave South, free North, and the open, unsettled West. Not many years before, western Missouri had been the scene of vicious wars between the Indian nations and white settlers, as well as riots and armed attacks that had driven out Mormon settlers from the East. On the Border, men carried guns and bowie knives as a way of life. With no railroads, the area was relatively isolated from the cities to the east, and the people enforced the law as they saw fit.

Robert and Zerelda James settled on a farm outside of Kearney, a small town in Clay County, where they became part of a tightly knit community of like-minded Southerners. They had been married less than a year, and the untamed Border seemed like a place with tremendous possibilities. An energetic, newly ordained Baptist minister, Robert James foresaw a great future in preaching to the settlers on the western frontier. His wife, Zerelda, was a proud and forceful woman with a long nose, a firmly set jaw, and large, fierce eyes. The two had met during Robert's years in seminary, while Zerelda attended school at a Roman Catholic convent, and they married soon after he was ordained.

The young couple flourished in northwestern Missouri. On January 10, 1843, Zerelda gave birth to her first child, a healthy boy she named Alexander Franklin James—known for the rest of his life as Frank. Robert James became pastor of the nearby New Hope Baptist Church, and the congregation quickly expanded under his guidance. He traveled constantly, preaching to revival meetings and new congregations that formed along the dirt roads of the Border. Soon he founded two additional churches, as well as the Liberty Baptist Association and a local Baptist college.

Seemingly tireless in his work for the church, Robert James possessed tremendous energy—but so did his outspoken wife. The marriage was sometimes turbulent, and there were rumors of arguments and quarrels. But the James family continued to prosper as the years passed. In addition to Robert's work as a minister, the couple labored on a farm that grew to 275 acres before the end of the decade, raising sheep, cattle, and horses. Their family continued to grow, too. A second son, Robert, died as an infant, but their third boy was born on September 5, 1847. They christened him Jesse Woodson James. Two years later, a little sister named Susan Lavenia joined the boys.

Robert was away much of the time in his work as a Baptist minister, so Zerelda was responsible for the farm even as she raised three children who were all too young to be of much help. She managed, however, in the same way as many of the wealthier families in Clay County: with the help of black slaves. By 1850, the James family had bought a total of seven slaves.

Few whites in Missouri actually owned slaves, but most of them approved of slavery. Seventy-five percent of the population of the state (including Robert and Zerelda James) had originally come from farther south, where slaveholding was a way of life, and it seemed like a perfectly natural system to most of them. Slavery, in fact, meant so much to Missourians that their first state constitution included a clause that required that *free* blacks be kept out of the state. Free black citizens, the state's founders thought, would be a bad influence on the slaves. Slavery grew into a big business in Missouri, and St. Louis emerged as a major center for the trade in human beings.

In the 1850s, though, tensions over slavery in Missouri began to rise. A wave of immigrants from Ireland and Germany flowed into the state, most of whom opposed slavery. New settlers from the free North, too, were coming to Missouri, including a few active abolitionists who campaigned for a complete end to slavery in the United States. By the end of the decade, slaves made up less than 10 percent of the state's population.

In Clay County, which had a higher proportion of slaves than most Missouri counties, Southerners like the James family worried that the new immigration would change Missouri's identity as a slave state. They resented the Northerners and foreign settlers as outsiders who threatened their way of life. Fistfights and even riots occasionally broke out between pro- and antislavery partisans. Wild rumors flew about "nigger stealing"—raids on farms by abolitionists trying to liberate slaves.

When Jesse James had just turned three another great wave of history swept his father away from home: the California gold rush of 1849. After gold was discovered at Sutter's Mill in California, thousands of gold hunters rushed by ship and by covered wagon to the streams and gold mines of California. Always eager to do the work of God, Robert James saw a new opportunity to preach to the settlers in the California mountains. With the same energy and restlessness that once took him from Kentucky to western Missouri, he set out in 1850 with a party of gold seekers heading west. He planned to stay a year or so, preaching and organizing Baptist churches on the West Coast before returning. He never came back. Only 32 years old, Robert James fell ill and died shortly after arriving in the California goldfields.

From this point on, the strong-willed Zerelda James became the dominant figure in the lives of Frank and Jesse. Yet their father left his mark on the young boys as well. A college-educated man with a sizable library (in a land where many could not even read), he left Frank with a taste for learning. Most of the legends surrounding Frank describe him as studious and well-read, fond of quoting Shakespeare. Jesse inherited strong religious beliefs from his minister father; even though he lived his entire adult life outside the law, he developed a reputation as a devout, churchgoing Christian.

Zerelda James now found herself a widow with a large farm and three children. Not long after Robert died, she

Frank and Jesse's mother, Zerelda, a powerful, determined woman, anchored the family after their father's death and provided a haven in Clay County to which they could retreat throughout their outlaw careers.

married Benjamin Simms. Always fiercely loyal to her sons, she left Simms after a few months because, according to a family story, she disliked the way he treated Frank and Jesse. Simms died not long after. Zerelda married again in September 1855, when Jesse was 8 and Frank was 12. Her new husband, Reuben Samuel, a doctor, had a quiet, steady manner. After two stormy marriages, Zerelda got along well with her new husband. Unlike Robert James, Dr. Samuel spent most of his time working on the farm with the family. He was kind to her three children, and the couple went on to have four more of their own: Archie, John, Sallie, and Fannie.

Dr. Reuben Samuel, Zerelda's third husband, was a quiet, steady man. Unlike her second husband, whom she left because she did not like the way he treated her boys, he did not try to interfere with the tight bond between Zerelda and her sons.

Growing up on a farm on the Border, Jesse and Frank learned to ride and care for horses and handle firearms; they also learned the details of the surrounding landscape—the neighbors' farms, the main and side roads, the woods, fields, and local towns. But their childhood and early teenage years were fairly quiet. In later years, after

they had won fame as outlaws, dozens of stories appeared in newspapers and dime novels about their adventures as children, but they spent most of their time in the 1850s working on the family farm, going to church, and growing up in the tightly knit community of Clay County.

Events across the western border, however, soon threw a shadow over the family. A national crisis erupted over the future of slavery—specifically, slavery in the Kansas-Nebraska Territory just west of Missouri. Breaking an old agreement under the Missouri Compromise of 1820 to keep Kansas and Nebraska free, Northern and Southern congressmen agreed to open the area to settlers and let them vote on whether their new states should be slave or free. The Kansas-Nebraska Act of 1854 started a furious race between the abolitionists of the North and the slaveholders of the South to settle Kansas.

The slaveholding politicians in Missouri led the rush to make Kansas a slave state. "We are playing for a mighty stake," said Missouri senator David Atchison. "If we win we carry slavery to the Pacific Ocean, if we fail we lose Missouri, Arkansas, Texas, and all the territories." The abolitionists were equally determined to halt the spread of slavery. They formed the New England Emigrant Aid Society to help antislavery settlers move to Kansas. From 1854 on, thousands of abolitionist pioneers flooded into Kansas, building towns and laying claims to farmland, far outnumbering the proslavery settlers from Missouri.

Across the Border region of western Missouri, panic spread as newspapers printed stories of slave-stealing raids by the Red Legs and Jay Hawks, or Jayhawkers, as the antislavery Kansans were nicknamed. Leading slaveholders like Senator Atchison decided to take matters into their own hands. They formed armed gangs, such as the Kickapoo Rangers and the Blue Lodges. Men from Clay County and elsewhere around the Border saddled up and rode into Kansas to terrorize the abolitionists. "We are organizing," Atchison told Secretary of War Jefferson

Davis. "We will be compelled to shoot, burn and hang, but the thing will soon be over." Nicknamed the Border Ruffians, these ruthless Missourians burned farms, ambushed settlers, and even attacked the abolitionist town of Lawrence. They also rode across the border to vote illegally in Kansas elections, putting the territory under the control of proslavery officials.

The entire nation exploded in outrage over "Bleeding Kansas," as the newspapers of the North called it. The antislavery Republican party, which in 1856 ran its first candidate for president, John C. Frémont, won new supporters all across the North among those infuriated at the terror wrought by the proslavery forces. On the other side, Southern politicians determined that Kansas had to become a slave state, whether the process was fair and democratic or not. The Jayhawkers formed their own military companies and fought back, led by men like Charles Jennison and the charismatic Jim Lane.

The warfare on the Border hung over the childhood of Jesse James, as he grew up in the heart of Border Ruffian territory with a mother who was fiercely proud of the South. The nation was on the verge of splitting in two over the fate of Bleeding Kansas. It would not be long before the conflict that was swallowing the nation engulfed his own life as well.

Drawn by a desire to attack and destroy all symbols of authority, William Clarke Quantrill switched sides in the guerrilla warfare of the border region to become a leading terrorist for the Confederate bushwhackers. Both James brothers rode with Quantrill's raiders at one time.

3

War

"A HOUSE DIVIDED AGAINST ITSELF cannot stand," Abraham Lincoln told a Republican party convention in 1858. "I believe this government cannot endure, permanently half *slave* and half *free*." But the leaders of the South warned that the government would *only* endure if it remained divided into slave and free sections. As Senator John Crittenden of Kentucky warned, the South had "come to the conclusion that in case Lincoln should be elected . . . she could not submit to the consequences, and therefore . . . will secede from the Union."

In the election of 1860, the people of Missouri voted for slavery—but not for secession from the Union. Four candidates ran for president that year. Abraham Lincoln, the Republican antislavery candidate, won the votes of the German settlers in Missouri (barely 10 percent of the total). At the other extreme was John C. Breckinridge, the candidate of the secessionists. Less than one out of five Missourians voted for Breckinridge. In between were the moderate Democrats Stephen A. Douglas and John Bell, who wanted to keep both slavery and the Union, and between the two they gathered 7 out of 10 votes in the state.

Frank James was a thoughtful, bookish man, reputedly fond of quoting Shakespeare; although he fought as a bushwhacker in the Civil War before Jesse did, afterward Frank may have been dragged reluctantly into the life of an outlaw by his hotheaded younger brother.

With the Democratic vote split nationwide among three candidates, Lincoln won the election. The Southern states immediately moved to secede, forming the Confederate States of America in February 1861. Governor Claiborne Fox Jackson of Missouri eagerly wanted to join the southern Confederacy. He was a rich slaveholder who had led the Border Ruffians in raids on Kansas. Jackson had the state legislature call a special convention to decide if the state should leave the Union. He also called for 50,000 volunteers to form a Home Guard to oppose the Union forces.

Unfortunately for Jackson, the men of Missouri responded with little enthusiasm. Not even 5,000 men enrolled in the new Home Guard, barely a tenth of the number he requested. But Clay County answered the call. In the town of Kearney a group of local young men organized a company for the Home Guard. Among them was 18-year-old Frank James.

When the special convention showed signs of voting for the Union, the governor and his men struck on their own. They began by seizing the federal arsenal in Liberty, and they made plans to capture the St. Louis arsenal. With these steps, Jackson and his supporters launched Missouri into four years of chaos.

A federal officer who had just arrived on the scene, however, outmaneuvered Jackson. Nathaniel Lyon, a New England Yankee, had helped put down the Border Ruffian attacks on Kansas and had earned a reputation as a tough antislavery fighter. Relying on troops recruited from the German immigrants, Lyon captured Jackson's men in St. Louis and drove back the rest of the secessionist forces. Frank James and the Clay County company retreated to the southwestern corner of the state along with the rest of Jackson's motley army.

Lyon's actions infuriated many people who had wanted to stay neutral in the war. By using the German settlers for troops, he made the American-born Missourians feel as if they were being suppressed by a foreign army. The situation grew worse when the German immigrant troops killed and wounded dozens of civilians during a riot in St. Louis. More Missourians rallied to the Confederate cause, including General Sterling Price, an experienced military man who took charge of the Southern troops. Governor Jackson and a handful of legislators who had fled St. Louis met at the Arkansas border and declared that Missouri had seceded and joined the Confederacy.

Despite the hopes of Zerelda Samuel and her boys, Governor Jackson's declaration carried little weight. As open war broke out between North and South with the Battle of Bull Run on July 21, 1861, the convention called to discuss secession declared itself the provisional state government and came out squarely for the Union. Meanwhile, Frank fought in the ferocious Battle of Wilson's Creek on August 10, 1861, where Lyon made a surprise attack on Price's Confederate army. At the end of the day, Lyon himself died in the fighting, and the Union army retreated from the field. General Price now quickly marched north, gathering new recruits along the way, and captured the town of Lexington, Missouri, and the 3,500 Union troops stationed there.

General Price, however, eventually had to retreat once again to northern Arkansas as his men trickled out of his army. Frank James himself fell sick and remained behind as the Southern army retreated to Arkansas. Many other local boys did the same, deserting Price's army and going back to their homes to help with the autumn harvest. The Southern army later made one last major attempt to recapture Missouri, an effort that ended in a crushing defeat at the Battle of Pea Ridge. The Union army now firmly held the state of Missouri in its grip.

But Pea Ridge proved to be only the beginning of the war in Missouri. Secret agents, such as Captain Joseph Shelby, stole into Missouri to recruit troops for the Confederacy and stir up trouble behind Union lines. Union officers worried about their ability to control the Southern sympathizers in the state. Already, on August 30, 1861, John C. Frémont (the new Union commander) had announced the death penalty for guerrillas and declared that the property of Confederate sympathizers would be seized and their slaves freed. Lincoln forced Frémont to rescind the order, but it had already angered many Missourians who had wanted to stay neutral in the war.

The worst was yet to come. From across the Kansas border rode regiments of Jayhawker cavalry, dressed now in Union blue and carrying federal-issue carbines. Ever since the last Border Ruffians had gone back to Missouri in the days of Bleeding Kansas, the antislavery Jayhawkers had been burning for revenge. Now that Lincoln had won the presidency, Kansas was a state, a free state; the gun-toting abolitionist Jim Lane was a senator with a great deal of power in Washington; and the Jayhawkers had enlisted to fight for the Union. These fiercely religious Kansans believed that God had commanded them to free every slave, exterminate every slaveholder, and destroy Missouri. When the Civil War broke out, Lane came home to head his own brigade of three regiments (Charles Jennison and James Montgomery, veteran fighters of the Bleeding Kansas era, also led cavalry units), and in the summer of 1861 "Lane's Brigade" crossed the border.

The Jayhawkers hailed Lane as a hero. One soldier described him as a dashing figure, "dressed in long-legged, high heeled boots, neat dress coat and sash and glazed cap, lacking only a plume to remind one of a brigand of the old times." The revenge of Lane and the other Jayhawkers would take a bloody form. Kansas Governor John J. Ingalls said of the Seventh Kansas Cavalry, "If there was *a band of destroying angels* in one congregation I saw them there. They take no prisoners and are not troubled with red tape sentimentalism in any form."

On September 23, 1861, Lane's men rode into Osceola, the county seat of St. Clair County, a town that had once been a supply depot for Price's Confederate army. They stripped the town and burned it down. Osceola marked only the beginning: the Kansas regiments marched across Missouri, torching farms, robbing homes, and torturing men for information on Southern sympathizers. "Jayhawking" became a new word on the Border, a term for looting and pillaging by soldiers of any persuasion.

Within a few months, the Kansas troops had laid waste to large stretches of western Missouri. In December 1861, John Martin, a Kansas officer, described what the Jayhawkers had done to Westport (a Missouri town near Kansas City): "Westport was once a thriving town, with large stores, elegant private dwellings, and a fine large hotel. Now soldiers are quartered in the dwellings and horses occupy the storerooms. The hotel was burned down three days ago. The houses are torn to pieces, plastering off, the mantles used to build fires, and doors unhinged. I presume the place will be burned as soon as the troops leave." In the countryside, he saw "crops ungathered, houses deserted, barns & stables falling to pieces, fences torn down and stock running loose and uncared for. . . . I have been all over the country about here without meeting with half a dozen habital dwellings." Even the regular Union officers began to worry about the destruction wrought by the Jayhawkers. The new commander in the West, General Halleck, wrote to Washington that they had "turned against us many thousands who were formerly Union men."

Halleck was right. Many of the men who had voted overwhelmingly in favor of moderate candidates in 1860 and for pro-Union men in the special convention election of 1861 now seethed with bitterness. As the Jayhawkers plundered indiscriminately through the Border counties, local men gathered into small groups to fight as guerrillas—sometimes commanded by regular Confederate officers, sometimes acting on their own. In the western counties especially, these guerrillas started bushwhacking (ambushing) Union troops, cutting telegraph lines, and burning bridges. In Jackson County, just south of Clay, a band formed in 1862 under the man who became the most infamous bushwhacker of all, William Clarke Quantrill.

Quantrill had been born in Ohio and had no particular ties to the South, but he did have a passion for killing and a gift for guerrilla tactics. A strange, charismatic man, he had actually been a Jayhawker himself during the Bleeding Kansas era (though his men did not know it), and he had spent some time with the native tribes in Indian Territory. In nearby Clay County, Frank and Jesse James soon heard tales of Quantrill's exploits—about how he and his men thundered out of the woods on the fastest horses in the Border, firing left and right with a revolver in each hand, then fading back into the bush before they could be caught. In the summer of 1862, Quantrill's raiders (including men who would become notorious guerrillas on their own, such as "Bloody Bill" Anderson, George Todd, and Cole Younger) won a series of spectacular victories over Union detachments, including the capture of Independence, Missouri, on August 11 and the Battle of Lone Jack on August 16.

Jesse James, however, was still too young to join the guerrillas in 1862, and Frank had already gone off once to do his duty for the South as a soldier. When the provisional state government offered an amnesty for ex-Confederate soldiers in April 1862, Frank went to Liberty to sign the papers and take an oath of allegiance to the United States. But on July 22, the provisional government ordered every adult man to join the state militia and fight for the Union. For the James-Samuel family, ordering Frank to fight against his fellow Southerners went too far. Frank refused to enlist in the militia, landed in jail, and then escaped and went to the bush to join a guerrilla band.

By early 1863, Frank James had joined a unit of bushwhackers, and by summer he rode with Quantrill himself. Like the hundreds of guerrillas fighting all across Missouri, he engaged in attacks on Union camps, sentries, and supply wagons; he ambushed patrols, cut telegraph lines, burned bridges—and burned down the homes of pro-Union civilians.

Jesse James stayed in close touch with his older brother while Frank was in the bush. Frank James and his fellow guerrillas occasionally hid on the family farm, where they got food, ammunition, and other supplies. Jesse and his mother worked as lookouts for the bushwhackers, sending word about the movements of Union troops and militia and carrying messages for the guerrillas. Before long, state militia and federal officers began to notice the activity on the Samuel farm.

On a summer day in 1863, while Jesse plowed in the field and his mother and stepfather worked in the house, soldiers from the state militia suddenly rode onto their farm. The militia's reputation was even worse than the Jayhawkers', and they were true to form that day. The troops stormed into the house, demanding information on Frank and the guerrillas. They dragged Dr. Samuel outside, put a noose around his neck, threw the rope over a tree, and pulled him up and down three times to make him talk, nearly strangling him. They surrounded Jesse's pregnant mother Zerelda, trying to bully her into telling them what she knew about the bushwhackers. Jesse learned of the raid when some of the militiamen appeared on the edge of the field. They chased him as he turned and ran, lashing his back as he tried to escape. Unable to get any information, the troops finally left empty-handed. Fifteen-year-old Jesse swore he would get even.

April 1863, when Jesse was 15 years old, the Missouri militia raided his family's farm to demand information about Frank James and Quantrill's guerrillas. They tortured Dr. Samuel, hanging him by the neck three times from the tree pictured here, but they could not make him talk.

Jesse James joined the Civil War as a Confederate bushwhacker when he was 16 years old. Already a southern sympathizer, Jesse's hatred of the Union soldiers increased after a raid on his family's farm in which he was lashed, his stepfather was tortured, and their farm was looted.

4

Under the Black Flag

THE ATTACK ON THE SAMUEL FARM made up only a small part of the destruction taking place on the Border. "This once beautiful and peaceful land is forsaken and desolated, ruined," a local man wrote from Clay County, "and only fit [for] bats, owls, and cockralls [cockerels] to inhabit." At the Samuel home, like so many others, Union troops had stolen what they wanted—horses, livestock, saddles, and food. Any slaves still on the Samuel farm when the war started had long since escaped, fleeing to the light of the Jayhawkers' campfires as they marched through the state.

"We are at war with those who were brothers, friends, neighbors," the Union command declared. "They are now enemies." Local men who sided with the Union led militia raids on their neighbors; bushwhackers burned out and murdered anyone who aided the Northern armies. No stranger could be trusted. Union troops sometimes disguised themselves as guerrillas to trick Southern sympathizers into revealing themselves, and the bushwhackers did the same thing, wearing captured blue Union uniforms as disguises. The Yankees usually shot the civilians they caught this way and torched their farms. The bushwhackers struck with special viciousness against the German immigrants and blacks; few survived an encounter with the guerrillas.

In August 1863, General Thomas C. Ewing, Jr., the Union commander in Kansas City, ordered the arrests of all the female relatives of the known Quantrill guerrillas. Behind Ewing's order lurked the powerful figure of Senator Jim Lane, who suffered acute embarrassment from the obvious failure of his brutal efforts to "loyalize" Missouri. Union troops took the women from their homes and jailed them in a three-story building in Kansas City. On August 14, the prison collapsed, killing five women and leaving several others with severe injuries. The sisters of Bill Anderson, one of Quantrill's leading lieutenants, and John McCorkle (a scout for the guerrillas) died in the disaster. The enraged bushwhackers believed that the federals had sabotaged the building. On August 18, General Ewing followed the catastrophe with General Order Number Ten, which banished many of the guerrillas' families from Missouri (the Samuel family did not fall under this order and remained in the state).

Quantrill decided to retaliate. His messengers carried word to his subordinates and men who had ridden with him in the past to gather in Johnson County for a special mission. Between 450 and 500 guerrillas, including many of the most notorious rebels in Missouri, answered the call.

Frank James rode to Johnson County in a unit led by Cole Younger. Younger was a massive man and a relentless killer. His father had actually been strongly pro-Union, but the Kansas Jayhawkers had looted and burned his farm anyway, murdering the old man before they left. Cole Younger joined the bushwhackers to get revenge, and now he commanded his own squad.

Quantrill told the assembled bushwhackers what he had in mind: to destroy Lawrence, the home of Jim Lane and the center of Jayhawker life in Kansas. He hoped to capture Lane himself and bring him back to Missouri for a lynching. For two days they rode across the plains toward their target. The guerrillas were a motley force, riding the finest horses on the Border and armed mainly with shotguns, bowie knives, and their favorite weapon of all, the Colt Navy revolver (so-called because the first model commemorated a Texas naval victory over the Mexicans). Many of them wore "guerrilla shirts"—homespun brown woolen shirts elaborately embroidered by their female relatives. As they rode deeper into Kansas, Quantrill kidnapped local farmers for guides, then shot them when their knowledge of the land ahead ran out.

Bob, Jim, and Cole Younger (from left to right) pose with their mother, Henrietta. Cole became a bushwhacker after Union troops killed his father and looted and burned his family's farm. After the war, the Youngers would become the core members of Jesse James's gang, which was often called the James-Younger gang. A fourth brother, John, was killed by the Pinkerton detectives.

Bill Anderson, a lieutenant for Quantrill and later the leader of his own guerrilla unit, was known as Bloody Bill because of the savagery of his tactics. His men took no prisoners, killing and often scalping and mutilating their victims. Jesse James fought alongside Anderson, and for a time Jesse's horse was bedecked with human scalps.

At dawn on August 21, 1863, Quantrill surveyed unsuspecting Lawrence, a quiet, well-ordered town of about 3,000 located far from the bloody fighting in Missouri and completely unprepared for the horror that was about to begin. After ordering the bushwhackers to kill every man and burn every building, with a wild yell the guerrilla commander led the charge down through the streets. Fanning out through the town, the Missourians pulled families from their homes, set fire to houses and businesses, dragged the men out in the open and shot them in front of their families. Frank James killed and looted as freely as the rest. Bill Anderson, however, wrought the worst mayhem of all. Enraged by the death of the women in Kansas City, Anderson killed with such fury that he was known as "Bloody Bill" for the rest of the war. All told, the guerrillas slaughtered between 150 and 200 civilians in the Lawrence streets as the town burned around them.

Jim Lane, however, escaped. The moment he heard the sounds of the attack, he ran from his house in his nightshirt and hid in a cornfield. The guerrillas started back to Missouri that same morning, pursued all the way by Union cavalry. They had hardly lost a man.

Kansas howled for revenge. Back in Clay County, Jesse and his family heard of the Lawrence massacre and fully expected retaliation from the Jayhawkers. Mr. A. Comingo from nearby Lexington wrote that "the people are crazy from fear and terror with which their lives are filled . . . weeping and wailing like children." Lincoln's administration warned Senator Lane that Union troops would stop any attempt at revenge on Missouri by the Kansans. But Jim Lane was a powerful man on the Border, and he practically ordered General Ewing to strike back.

On August 25, 1863, Ewing issued General Order Number Eleven. The order commanded all people living in Jackson, Cass, Bates, and half of Vernon counties, all of which lined the Kansas border, to leave their homes immediately. Thousands of Missourians—Unionists and secessionists alike—fled in terror. Union soldiers marched through the area, destroying it so thoroughly that it became known as the Burnt District. They burned crops, stripped fences of rails and posts, tore apart and torched houses and barns, and killed or drove off the livestock.

The time of the black flag descended on Missouri. No longer would the state government offer amnesty, as it had to Frank James in 1862; nor would the guerrillas parole their prisoners (letting them go free on the promise that they would not fight again) as Quantrill did in the first year of the war. After the horrors of Lawrence and General Order Number Eleven, Union cavalry and Southern guerrillas began to fly black banners as they rode into battle, promising no surrender and no prisoners. The war on the Border became a war of extermination.

In the manhunt following the Lawrence massacre, the state militia struck the Samuel farm again, this time arresting the pregnant Zerelda Samuel and putting her in jail in St. Joseph, along with one of her younger children. Jesse James—like Cole Younger, Bill Anderson, and so many other guerrillas—wanted revenge.

Quantrill and most of his lieutenants, however, had ridden to Texas. While the bushwhackers spent the winter in Sherman, Texas, a bitter feud broke out between Bloody Bill Anderson and Quantrill. The two grew so angry with each other that Bloody Bill and his men left to set up their own camp. Other lieutenants also lost confidence in Quantrill's leadership. Before the winter ended, George Todd effectively took command of Quantrill's own unit.

Frank James, however, remained loyal to Quantrill. He also met and became close friends with regular Confederate officers who admired Quantrill, including General Joseph Shelby and Major John Newman Edwards. Shelby, who had led Border Ruffian raids on Kansas before the war, had emerged as a dashing, innovative cavalry officer. Since the Battle of Wilson's Creek he had led a number of daring raids and recruiting missions in Missouri, accompanied by Edwards, a former newspaperman who was his adjutant. Now he commanded a hardbitten unit of 600 men known as the Iron Brigade—perhaps the finest cavalry outfit in the Confederate army west of the Mississippi. Shelby and Edwards admired Frank James, and they began a friendship that would last long after the war.

In March 1864, the guerrillas broke camp and started the march north. Quantrill rode along, but now the men were following the lead of George Todd and Bloody Bill Anderson, who each led a column back into Missouri. The Union forces in the state, after a long, quiet winter, were completely unprepared for the return of the bushwhackers. Breaking into small groups, the guerrillas launched a series of fierce attacks on federal posts and ambushed unsuspecting Union troops across the state.

At last, Jesse had his chance to join the fight. Heading into the bush at the first word of the guerrillas' return, he joined a squad led by Fletch Taylor, one of Bill Anderson's lieutenants. Jesse was only 16 years old, but he quickly picked up the ways of the bushwhackers. He learned how to keep steady on a horse as he rode at breakneck speed with the reins in his teeth and a revolver in each hand, how to snap off an accurate shot without taking time to aim. The guerrillas taught him how to pack his own powder charge for each pistol shot: Union troops used prepackaged gunpowder, but the bushwhackers discovered that a smaller charge kept the pistol from jumping when it fired, giving better accuracy. He discovered the importance of keeping four or even six Navy revolvers on his body, to save the time needed to reload during battle. He learned quickly. Before long, Bloody Bill himself said, "Not to have any beard, he is the keenest and cleanest fighter in the command."

Frank James, nicknamed "Buck" by the other guerrillas, had a reputation as a quiet, solid man, especially good for

*Confederate guerrillas
Frank (center) and Jesse
James (right) pose with Fletch
Taylor in approximately 1864.
Taylor, a lieutenant under
"Bloody Bill" Anderson, led a
squad of terrorists that Jesse
joined at the age of 16.*

duties like scouting that required close attention and steady
nerves. But Jesse stood out as a ferocious fighter with a
quick sense of humor, an excellent shot who loved to be in
the thick of the fighting. He was still just a teenager,
though, and the other men would not let him forget it. In
June 1864, not long after he joined Fletch Taylor's guerrillas, Jesse took part in a fight in Clay County, helping to
kill two local pro-Union men from the Bigelow family.
During the fighting, Jesse apparently shot off the tip of his

own finger and shouted "Dingus!" According to legend, his choice of words so amused the hard-swearing bushwhackers that they nicknamed him "Dingus" for the rest of the war.

While Frank remained loyal to Quantrill's original band, fighting under Todd and later again under Quantrill himself, Jesse rode with Bloody Bill, the most savage of any of the guerrilla captains. Anderson's men never took prisoners, and they became notorious for mutilating Union dead. Scalping—removing the hair and skin from the top of a man's head—became standard practice in Bloody Bill's band. The most infamous of all of Anderson's men was Archie Clement, a short, almost illiterate fighter nicknamed the "Executioner" because of his pride in killing and scalping prisoners. Clement even left clumsily written notes on the bodies of dead Union soldiers, claiming credit for killing and scalping them.

Jesse took part in Anderson's raids and ambushes along the border between Ray and Carroll counties until the middle of August 1864, when a bullet from a Union pistol tore through the right side of his chest. No one expected him to live for more than a few days. Anderson left him in the care of John A. Rudd, a Confederate supporter in Carroll County. Against heavy odds, Jesse survived. Rudd's family nursed him back to health, and he revived with remarkable speed. Within a month he climbed back in the saddle to ride again with Bloody Bill—only now with an ugly scar under his guerrilla shirt.

On September 26, 1864, Jesse and Frank James were temporarily reunited when Todd and Anderson set up camp with their men in some woods in Boone County, about four miles south of the town of Centralia, Missouri. Together the two groups of bushwhackers had about 200 men. Anderson and Todd, however, could not agree on what to do. Bloody Bill argued that they should attack Centralia, but Todd refused to take part. Disgusted, Anderson ordered his men to follow him into town, leaving Todd's guerrillas behind.

For almost three hours, Jesse, Archie Clement, and the rest of Bloody Bill's men shot up Centralia, robbed the townspeople, and torched the railroad depot. On Anderson's orders, the men piled railroad ties on the tracks to stop any trains that might come along while they looted the town. At noon the train from St. Charles pulled to a stop at the pile of heavy wood ties. Shooting and yelling, the guerrillas ordered everyone off the train and discovered 35 Union troops on board. The federal soldiers were traveling home from the front on leave, and were completely unarmed. Anderson ordered them stripped, and his men took their uniforms for later use as disguises.

After this was done, he ordered the senior Union soldier, a sergeant named Thomas Goodman, separated from the rest, and he told Archie Clement to "muster out" the Union troops. Clement drew a pistol and began shooting the defenseless, nearly naked men; Jesse and the others joined in. Soon all but Goodman lay dead on the Centralia streets, and Bloody Bill's men went to work scalping and mutilating the bodies with their bowie knives. Then they cleared the tracks, set fire to the train, and ordered the engineer to start the engine. The burning train rolled down the tracks out of town, where it stopped after a few miles (the engineer had been careful to leave the valve on the boiler open). Satisfied with their work, the bushwhackers then rode back to join Todd with Goodman as their only prisoner.

Back at the camp, Todd argued with Anderson about the massacre, but time for debate had already run out. Confederate sentries reported the approach of hundreds of Union troops, flying the black flag as they rode out of Centralia. They were mounted infantry of the state militia, under the command of Major A. V. E. Johnson. After seeing the massacre in Centralia, Johnson had raised the black flag and sworn he would kill every last bushwhacker.

The guerrillas scattered to their horses as Todd and Anderson ordered them into a rough line facing the approaching Union soldiers, who soon rode into view and came to a halt. As the two lines of horsemen faced each other, the guerrilla commanders told their men to dismount and tighten their horses' saddle girths in preparation for battle. Believing the guerrillas intended to fight on foot, Major Johnson told his men to dismount as well, and every fourth man led away the horses of the others. The guerrillas, though, remained by their horses; when the enemy's animals had been taken off the field, they quickly remounted and charged, screaming wildly and shooting with deadly accuracy as they rode down on the Union line.

John McCorkle, who fought beside Frank and Jesse James that day, wrote that Johnson's men "stampeded in all directions, some of them running for their horses and some of them starting for Centralia afoot. We followed them into the town of Centralia, which was about three miles away, dealing death at every jump." McCorkle and Frank charged the panicking Union troops, firing at the running soldiers, until they met up with a company of Union infantry. Frank declared, "Hold on, boys, we've killed enough of them; let's go back," and they rode back to join the others. There they learned that Jesse had led the charge of Bloody Bill Anderson's men, heading straight for Major Johnson and shooting him down with his Colt revolver.

Out of about 175 Union troops, only those who had been holding the horses for the others escaped—barely 50 men. After the guerrillas left, Lieutenant Colonel Daniel Draper arrived with more federal troops and found the field littered with 124 Union dead. Draper sent a report back to his commander that described the condition of the bodies found beside the railroad tracks in Centralia: "Most of them were beaten over the head, seventeen of them were scalped, and one had his privates cut off and placed in his mouth. Every man was shot in the head. One man had his nose cut off." Bloody Bill's men had carefully shot every man to make sure he was dead, and then collected souvenirs from the remains with their knives. Jesse was now a month short of his 17th birthday.

The guerrillas as a whole had only a few weeks before an enormous disaster would overtake them all, a disaster brought on by General Sterling Price. Price, the Confederate hero of Wilson's Creek, had convinced the Confederate high command that he could invade Missouri from Arkansas with his ragged army, capture St. Louis before the Union could respond, and then retake Missouri for the South. With little to lose after the fall of Vicksburg, Jefferson Davis's government gave Price its approval. On September 19, 1864, Price launched his invasion, crossing the border between Arkansas and Missouri with 12,000 men. Joseph Shelby and his Iron Brigade of cavalry led the way as they marched north.

Times had changed, though, since the heady days when Price had won the Battle of Wilson's Creek. Price himself weighed about 300 pounds and had to be carried on a wagon pulled by 4 mules. Apart from some of the cavalry, including the Iron Brigade, Price's poorly equipped army scarcely looked any better. But this ragged force and its bloated general marched north with high expectations. On September 27, the same day as the massacre at Centralia, Price found his path blocked by General Ewing camped with a few hundred Union troops on a fortified hill known as Pilot Knob. Overriding Shelby's objections, Price attacked the entrenched defenders of the fort, losing 1,500 men in the carnage. Ewing held on and evacuated safely during the night. The disaster at Pilot Knob convinced Price that he could never capture St. Louis, which had far heavier fortifications. Instead, he swerved northwest, aiming at Jefferson City.

Price's orders disgusted Shelby. He and his men traveled light and fast and took risks, and General Price did not look ready to do either. Then Price decided to bypass Jefferson City, taking his army around the capital's fortresses and marching northwest along the Missouri River.

Despite the bloody fiasco at Pilot Knob and the decision to avoid both St. Louis and Jefferson City, the southerners of western Missouri hailed General Price as a conquering

General Joseph Shelby commanded a hard-bitten group of 600 men known as the Iron Brigade, one of the finest cavalry units in the Confederate army. Frank and Jesse James both served under Shelby, as did Major John Newman Edwards, Shelby's adjutant. Edwards, a newspaperman, later became the chief apologist for the James gang.

savior, come to rescue them from the Jayhawkers and the state militia. Young men flocked to the army as volunteers, and Price distributed rifles to as many as he could as he marched slowly up the river toward Kansas City.

Hundreds of other young men joined General Price as well—men who were already well armed with revolvers and shotguns. Guerrilla bands rode from all over the state to aid the great invasion. At Waverly, east of Lexington, Price welcomed George Todd and the rest of Quantrill's bushwhackers (including Frank James) and assigned them to Shelby's Iron Brigade as scouts.

Then, two weeks after the battles of Centralia and Pilot Knob, Jesse James rode into the Confederate camp with Bloody Bill Anderson and his men. Price's soldiers watched as the bushwhackers cantered past on their splendid horses, with bloody human scalps hanging from the bridles. General Price refused to deal with Anderson until he got rid of the scalps. The men disposed of their trophies, and Bloody Bill presented the general with a gift of silver-mounted pistols. The general accepted the gift, and the bushwhackers joined his army. Now all the main guerrilla forces had linked up with the Confederate invaders.

General Price appeared to be growing stronger with every step. On October 19, Shelby (now leading the guerrillas, including Frank and Jesse James, as well as his own Iron Brigade) attacked a Union force under General Blunt in Lexington. Jesse took part in the fighting as the horsemen forced Blunt out of Lexington, and in further skirmishing they pushed the Federals across the Big Blue River, south of Clay County. On October 22, 1864, Shelby and other cavalry generals smashed Blunt's line of Kansas militia. It looked as if Price would destroy the Union forces protecting Kansas.

But as was so often the case in the war in Missouri, appearances were deceiving. Fresh Union troops marched swiftly from the east, rapidly catching up with the slow-moving Confederate army. On the same day that Shelby's men tore apart Blunt's militiamen, 4,000 cavalry of the U.S. Army, under the command of Major General Alfred Pleasonton, launched a fierce attack on Price from the rear. Even more Union troops followed close behind. In fact, Pleasonton's hammer in the east would soon crush Price against the anvil of Blunt's position west of the Big Blue.

As Price pondered what to do next, the Confederate cavalry under generals Shelby, Fagan, and Marmaduke made one last attack on Blunt's force at Westport. More than 29,000 men fought for more than two hours in a wild battle that rolled back and forth. Jesse James and the other guerrillas fought with the Iron Brigade as Shelby drove back Blunt's more numerous troops. But then Pleasonton's Union cavalry suddenly appeared on the Confederate right and launched a fierce attack. The Federals crushed Marmaduke's division, forcing Shelby and Fagan back.

The battle became a rout. Price had already begun to retreat with the rest of his army when Pleasonton's attack destroyed most of his cavalry. The Confederates rushed south along the Missouri-Kansas border, abandoning wagons of loot and even guns and rifles as the Federals hounded their every step.

Another disaster soon followed for the guerrillas. Only a day or two after the Battle of Westport, Bloody Bill Anderson and his men rode straight into a Union ambush set by Major S. P. Cox. The infamous bushwhacker had finally been bushwhacked himself. Cox's force killed Anderson, along with a number of his men. Jesse James, Archie Clement, and a few others managed to escape.

On November 7, 1864, Price's army, only a fraction of the size it had been two months before, crossed the Arkansas River to safety. The invasion had rained disaster on the guerrillas of Missouri. By joining Price's regular army, they allowed themselves to be wiped out in the major battles on the Big Blue and the retreat south. This period of regular warfare decimated all the major guerrilla outfits and killed some of their most important leaders (in addition

Like many bushwhackers, Bloody Bill Anderson did not survive the disastrous alliance between the small, mobile guerrilla bands and the plodding Confederate army led by the unimaginative General Sterling Price. Price's invasion of Missouri ended in the massacre of his regular army and their guerrilla recruits, including Anderson. This photograph was taken after Anderson was killed in an ambush in 1864.

to Bloody Bill Anderson, the bushwhackers lost George Todd during fighting in Lexington on October 19).

Jesse James, however, continued to fight with the main Confederate army after its retreat to Arkansas. On November 12, 1864, he helped ambush a Kansas unit out jayhawking near Cane Hill and killed the enemy commander, Lieutenant Emmett Goss. Not long after, he rode south to Texas for the winter with a group that included Archie Clement and Bloody Bill's brother, Jim Anderson.

Frank James stayed behind in Missouri. After the death of George Todd, Quantrill reemerged to take command of his old outfit. With about 40 men, including Frank, Quantrill rode east for one last special mission—to assassinate President Abraham Lincoln. They got no farther than Kentucky. There they fell into an ambush sprung by Captain Edward Terrill in early May 1865. Terrill's men shot Quantrill to death, but Frank and a few others survived and surrendered to Union forces on July 26, 1865.

Jesse endured a dismal winter in Texas as the Confederate cause crumbled across the South. Union general William Tecumseh Sherman ravaged a broad swath of Georgia with his cataclysmic "march to the sea," then turned north and wrought even worse destruction in South Carolina. In January, Union forces closed off the last Confederate seaport. At Petersburg, Virginia, General Ulysses S. Grant steadily closed the ring around General Robert E. Lee's Army of Northern Virginia. When spring arrived, Jesse James and the few remaining guerrillas rode back north to Missouri, unaware that Lee had made his final surrender at Appomattox Courthouse.

The war was over, but it had changed Missouri almost beyond recognition. Jesse James discovered that his entire family had disappeared, banished from the state in a final act of vengeance against the guerrillas by the Union forces. His mother, Dr. Samuel, and their children had moved to Rulo, Nebraska, just across the river from Missouri. Many of their friends and neighbors had been killed or burned out by Union troops, state militiamen, or guerrillas. Most of the western half of the state was in ruins, from burned farms and fields overrun with weeds to destroyed bridges and displaced families.

Thousands of regular Southern troops had surrendered safely, but Jesse could not be sure that he would receive the same treatment. During the war the Union troops had shot bushwhackers on sight; on top of that, he had belonged to the most hated of all the guerrilla outfits. Archie Clement and Jim Anderson weighed the odds and decided to remain in hiding, but Jesse had a harder choice. He had a family that needed him badly in the tragic aftermath of the war. In June 1865, he and a small group of bushwhackers raised a white flag and rode into Lexington, Missouri, to surrender. Jesse James's war had come to an end.

General Robert E. Lee's surrender to General Ulysses S. Grant at Appomattox Courthouse in Virginia, shown above, ended the organized southern resistance in the Civil war. Jesse James's surrender did not go as smoothly as Lee's; he was shot in the chest and nearly killed while offering the white flag to Union troops.

5

Surrender and Survival

ON A JUNE DAY IN 1865, a handful of men slowly walked their horses along a dirt road into Lexington, Missouri. Like the Confederates at Appomattox Courthouse, they rode in silence to surrender to the Yankees, carrying the white flag of defeat. None felt more dejected than the teenage guerrilla they called Dingus, known to his mother as Jesse Woodson James.

To the Union garrison in Lexington, though, these bushwhackers bore no resemblance to the Southern soldiers who had served under Robert E. Lee or in any of the other regular Confederate armies. A group of Union troopers who saw them approach the town rode toward them, weapons drawn. Lead snapped in the air around the guerrillas as they wheeled their horses about in confusion. Jesse's horse fell dead from a shot, and as Jesse jumped clear he caught a bullet in his chest. The bushwhackers scattered, turning to fire back as they galloped away. One of them quickly pulled the wounded Jesse up behind him and rode after the others.

Jesse, however, could not endure the horse's jolting pace because of the pain from his wound. Rather than risk his friend's life, he slipped off the saddle and crawled into the dense woods nearby. Two of the Union soldiers saw what happened and turned off the road after him. As they approached his hiding spot in the brush, he pulled his Colt revolvers and opened fire. Now it was a Union trooper's turn to jump clear as one of Jesse's bullets dropped his horse. The two scrambled away to safety, and Jesse crawled deeper into the woods.

Feverish from his wound, Jesse spent the night in the brush hiding from the Union soldiers. The next morning he crawled into the field of a nearby farm and was found by a farmer who had been a Confederate sympathizer. The man took the wounded teenager to his house for a few days and then carried him to a local doctor. The physician did his best, but Jesse James lingered close to death, the bullet lodged in his chest.

Somehow, Jesse—still suffering badly from his wound—got to his mother and stepfather's farm in Rulo, Nebraska, where he stayed for two months. His stepfather treated him faithfully but he could do little for Jesse's badly infected wound. As his mother sat by his bed, Jesse begged her to take him back to Missouri rather than let him die in a Northern state. Zerelda James Samuel had bred her love of the South deep into her son. She agreed to take him back to Missouri to die.

Soon Zerelda and her boy were on a boat sailing down the Missouri River to Missouri. In the town of Harlem, just north of Kansas City, they stopped at a boardinghouse run by Zerelda's sister-in-law by her first marriage, Mrs. John Mimms. The Mimms family, believing Jesse to be dying, carried him to a room where they could comfort him during his last days. He was comforted most by his teenage cousin, Zerelda (who was named after his own mother).

To everyone's surprise, Jesse began to recover under his cousin's care. As he slowly regained his health, the two spent long hours together. He nicknamed her Zee, and his good spirits and sense of humor returned as they talked. Soon they fell in love. Even though they were teenagers and first cousins, they promised to marry each other someday.

Meanwhile, the Union generals started to relax their ironhanded rule of Missouri as the last surviving guerrillas surrendered. Starting in the summer of 1865, the military gradually lifted the strict measures the Union had used to suppress the guerrillas and their supporters. Zerelda learned that she and her husband would be allowed to return with their family to the farm in Clay County. Leaving Jesse in the care of the Mimms family, she returned to Nebraska to prepare for the move back to their old Missouri home.

Eventually Jesse was well enough to be put in a cart and carried back to Clay County. Frank had come home after his release by the federal authorities in Kentucky, and Dr. Samuel, Zerelda, and his brothers and sisters had returned from Nebraska as well. But they found the farm in ruins. Jesse still could not walk, and the black slaves who had once helped work the farm had long since been freed.

Frank and Dr. Samuel went to work rebuilding the place as Jesse slowly recuperated. The wound still bothered him, but he eventually took to his feet again. Every Sunday he made the journey to the nearby town of Kearney to attend the Baptist church. There the teenage boy—already an experienced killer—sang in the choir and underwent a baptism. Both Jesse and Frank lived quietly at home for the rest of 1865, as Union troops emptied the Missouri garrisons and returned to their home states.

The state government, however, followed a policy of revenge against former Confederates like the James-Samuel family. In 1865 the provisional state government called a special convention to draw up a new constitution for Missouri. Meeting in St. Louis, the convention quickly fell under the control of the Radical Republicans (the most

This photograph, discovered in a saloon in New Mexico, purportedly shows Jesse (left) and Frank James posing with their mother, Zerelda Samuel.

extreme, anti-Southern branch of Lincoln's party), led in Missouri by Charles D. Drake. The Drake faction cared little for reconciliation; they wanted revenge.

The new constitution they created all but banished former Confederates from public life in Missouri. Known as the Draconian Code, it imposed a "severe and searching" loyalty oath on all citizens. Under this oath, Missourians had to swear that they had never committed any of 86 specific acts in support of the South—including such activities as simply expressing sympathy for the Confederacy. Those who failed to take the oath lost the right to vote, serve as jurors, or practice their professions.

For the former Confederates in Missouri, the minority of Radical Republicans in control of the state replaced the Union army as their enemy. Across the state, those who had stayed loyal to the Union organized into armed gangs and took revenge on the former bushwhackers and their supporters, while the Republican-appointed courts and law officers looked the other way. Even church ministers who had supported the South suffered threats and harassment that drove them out of their congregations. And now that the judges were all Radical Republicans, Union men began to sue former Confederates for wartime attacks and abuse.

Across the South, the postwar era of Reconstruction put Radical Republican governments in power, bringing dramatic changes to states that had always been deeply conservative. But the war changed Missouri in more areas than just government. The fighting left the Border region so thoroughly devastated that one historian has called it simply "the Wasteland." At least 300,000 Missourians (roughly 1 out of every 3 persons) had fled or were driven out of the state during the war, leaving behind large tracts of abandoned farmland. Now that slavery was abolished, blacks left in large numbers. County governments (controlled, of course, by Radical Republicans) sold off the abandoned farms to immigrants from Northern states who crowded into Missouri after the end of the war. Almost 200,000 people moved into the state between 1865 and 1870, and nearly all of them came from the North (Illinois and Ohio in particular).

In Clay County, however, the Southerners held firm. Before the war, Clay had been a major center of slaveholding (more than one out of four people had been slaves). The white people of Clay had done all they could to support the guerrillas. With the end of the war, many who had been banished (like Dr. Samuel and his family) returned. They stood up to the Radical Republicans, often gathering in mobs and threatening the ruling officials.

As the election of 1866 approached, the Clay County voter registration supervisor, the court clerk, the sheriff, and the former militia captain feared for their lives. They asked the Union commander at Fort Leavenworth, Kansas, for soldiers to protect them: "We deem the lives of Union men in great danger," they wrote. "Several of the most respectable citizens have been ordered to leave and many others have been publicly insulted and their lives threatened. An armed mob consisting of the most dangerous men in the county numbering more than a hundred men resisted the Sheriff [while he was] attempting to arrest a man."

As former guerrillas, Jesse and Frank James probably took part in this local resistance to the Radical Republicans. They kept in touch with former bushwhackers, and they may have joined the group of about 100 ex-guerrillas who rode into nearby Lexington on election day to literally steal the election at gunpoint. Governor Fletcher responded by sending in the state militia. The militiamen, however, behaved far worse than the former bushwhackers, murdering and robbing the citizens and arresting a newspaper publisher who criticized them. The local population (who were mostly Southern sympathizers) had to ask for federal troops to protect them from the state militia. Peace returned when three companies of the U.S. Army marched in and drove the militiamen out.

In these angry, disjointed times, Jesse and Frank carried their pistols everywhere. Men roamed the countryside, settling old scores and robbing their neighbors. The Samuel family struggled desperately; the new state constitution prevented Dr. Samuel from practicing his profession, so he and his stepsons tried to rebuild the ruined farm with hard work and little money.

Sometime in early 1866, probably in January, some of Frank James's old friends from Quantrill's raiders met with him to suggest a solution to his troubles. About a dozen former bushwhackers had decided that the Clay County Savings Bank in Liberty was in need of robbing. The James boys' cousins Donny and Bud Pence formed part of the group, along with Oliver Shepherd and probably Oliver's brother George (George had led Jesse on the march to Texas in the winter of 1864). No one had ever robbed a bank in daylight before, except during a raid carried out by Confederate soldiers on a mission in the Civil War. According to legend, Frank agreed to join, but Jesse was physically still too weak.

On February 13, 1866, a blustery winter day, a dozen armed men rode into Liberty and took up key positions around the Clay County Savings Bank. Two men, wearing long military overcoats, walked into the bank and asked the cashier for change for a large bill. Then the two drew their revolvers and jumped over the counter, forcing the bank employees into the vault. They filled the large grain sack they carried with gold, silver, and paper currency, slammed the door on the two victims, and ran outside.

Out on the street, the robbers spurred their horses, shouting and firing their revolvers in the air. As they galloped out of town, George Wymore, a student from William Jewell College, wandered into their path. Yelling at him to get out of the way, the bank robbers shot him dead as they thundered past. The men of Liberty quickly formed a posse and chased after the bandits as they rode south toward the Missouri River. The outlaws, however, took a ferry across the river and lost their pursuers in a blizzard that swept blinding snow across the terrain.

The Liberty bank robbery marked a turning point for Jesse James. Even though there is no hard evidence that either Jesse or Frank took part, they certainly knew many of the bandits quite well. The crime netted more than $60,000 for the raiders, and it proved a major embarrassment for the local Republican officials.

Despite all the suffering and bitterness of Reconstruction Missouri, Jesse James might well have been able to live a quiet, peaceful life. But as a ferocious teenage boy on the war-torn Border he had grown accustomed to action and violence. At this point in his life, he did nothing with more skill than ride and shoot. At age 18, he saw in the Liberty raid a chance to do something more interesting than work the family farm. He never looked back.

The robbery of the Clay County Savings Bank in Liberty, Missouri, marked the beginning of the James gang's crime spree. A group of ex-bushwhackers, including several friends and relatives of the James brothers and possibly Frank James (Jesse was probably still recovering from a gunshot wound), robbed the bank in 1866.

More than any other person, Major John Newman Edwards was responsible for creating the myth that the James boys were heroic redeemers of the pride of the South. Edwards published countless editorials and letters in his newspaper claiming that Frank and Jesse James either were innocent, or that, like Robin Hood, they committed crimes only out of a selfless devotion to justice.

6

With the Younger Brothers

WHEN THE LIBERTY BANK ROBBERY took place in 1866, Frank James was 23 years old and Jesse was only 18. Neither of them had been leaders during their years as guerrillas. Even so, the older men in this loose group of ex-bushwhackers welcomed the James boys along as they planned the next raid.

On October 30, 1866, the robbers struck again, this time in Lexington, Missouri. At noon, three men took positions outside the Alexander Mitchell and Company bank as two others walked in. One of the two, a tall young man with a quick laugh, joked with the cashier and asked him to cash a $50 government bond. The cashier, a man named J. L. Thomas, started to explain that the bank did not buy that type of bond when two more men walked in with pistols in their hands. The gunmen stuffed more than $2,000 from the cash drawer into a grain sack, but failed to find the key to the vault when Thomas refused to help. The men quietly mounted their horses and rode out of town. The townspeople organized a posse to chase the bandits, but the posse fell under the leadership of Dave and John Pool—former guerrillas who had fought alongside both Frank and Jesse. The Pool brothers soon returned empty-handed.

By the time of the Lexington raid, the James brothers probably rode with the gang. Jesse, now recovered from his wound, may well have been the young man who had joked with the cashier. Young as he was, Dingus had a ferocious reputation with the other former guerrillas, and he made a natural recruit for their band.

On March 2, 1867, the gang struck again. Six men rode into Savannah, Missouri, and demanded that Judge John McClain open the vault of his bank. When McClain refused, the bandits opened fire and left him for dead. The gang got nothing, and McClain survived his wounds.

After their failure at Savannah, the former bushwhackers met to plan a more spectacular raid—on the Hughes and Wasson Bank in Richmond, just east of Clay County. About a dozen men gathered for the robbery, including many of Frank James's old friends from Quantrill's band: Payne Jones, Andy McGuire, Thomas Little, and Allen Parmer. A new man came along as well—Cole Younger, Frank's old commander in the massacre at Lawrence. Younger had been sent on a mission to California after the Lawrence raid, where he stayed until after the war ended. After returning to Missouri, he had rejoined his old comrades.

On May 22, 1867, the men rode into Richmond in small groups, each taking a different street as they converged on the town square. Four of them dismounted and went inside; with the help of their Colt revolvers, they collected more than $4,000 in their wheat sack. But the eight or so who waited outside—heavily armed and on horseback— aroused the suspicions of the townspeople. Across the square, local men ran to get their guns.

The outlaws had been shot at many times before, and as the men of Richmond opened fire on them they coolly fired back. One of the gang shot the mayor, John Shaw. Another saw a young man named Frank Griffin hiding behind a tree in front of the courthouse with an army carbine, and he killed Griffin with a shot to the forehead. As the four bandits emerged from the bank and leapt on their horses, Griffin's elderly father ran forward. One of the gang put his pistol to the man's head and fired, then shot him again as he lay on the ground to make sure that he was dead.

The townspeople quickly formed a posse that rode hard after the fleeing bandits. That night the posse got close enough to engage in a brief gunfight, but the gang broke up into small groups and fled into the dense woods off the road.

In the months that followed the robbery and killings, the enraged people of Richmond took justice into their own hands. A few days after the robbery, a mob of local people broke into the jail and hung a horse thief named Felix Bradley, who—rumor had it—had known about the raid ahead of time. In late May, Missouri lawmen captured Thomas Little and threw him into the Johnson County jail in Warrensburg. While he waited to go to court, a crowd of men broke into his cell, held a mock trial, and lynched him. Two other suspects, Payne Jones and Dick Burns, were murdered a month or so afterward. Later that year, the St. Louis police arrested Andy McGuire and sent him to Richmond together with another suspect named James Devers. On March 17, 1868, a dozen citizens broke into the jail and hung them both.

As the year 1867 went by, almost half of the gang who had been in Richmond were rounded up or murdered. The others, including the James boys, tried to live quietly until the commotion blew over. Meanwhile, Bud Pence (who had settled in Nelson County, Kentucky, with his brother Donny) was arrested in Kentucky for the Liberty robbery. When the local sheriff heard about the lynchings in Missouri, however, he allowed Bud to escape.

With the older members of the gang lynched or locked up, Jesse and Frank James took on more of a leadership role in the band. But Missouri had clearly grown more dangerous for the outlaws over the preceding year. In early 1868, Bud Pence suggested to Jesse and Frank that Kentucky might make a better hunting ground. His brother Donny, in fact, could offer them some protection in his job as the sheriff of Nelson County. Cole Younger agreed. As a guerrilla, he had spent some time in Kentucky, and he claimed the banks were rich and fairly easy to rob.

In early March 1868, about a half dozen members of the gang—including Oliver and George Shepherd, who had fought alongside Jesse during the war—met at a hotel in Chaplin, Kentucky. Cole Younger reported that he had scouted out the town of Russellville, Kentucky, posing as a cattle buyer, and he thought the Nimrod Long bank would make a good target.

In March 1868, Jesse James and his gang robbed the Southern Bank of Kentucky in Russellville, shown here. Nimrod Long, the proprietor, escaped through the window with only a minor wound.

The gang saddled up and rode the hundred miles to Russellville, where they filled a cotton grain sack with more than $12,000 in Nimrod Long's bank. After a brief struggle, a bullet grazed Mr. Long as he escaped through a window. The bandits rode back to Chaplin unharmed.

Nimrod Long, however, hired D. G. Bligh, a private detective from Louisville, to investigate the robbery. Bligh passed along what he discovered to lawmen in Jackson County, Missouri, who promptly raided the farm of Oliver and George Shepherd. Oliver opened fire on the arresting officers, who shot him dead with a volley of lead. George, however, had left home for Kentucky, where the lawmen eventually tracked him down. George Shepherd stood trial for the Russellville robbery and eventually served three years in prison for the crime. Bligh suspected Cole Younger and the James brothers as well, though he never succeeded in having any of them arrested.

After the death of Oliver Shepherd and the capture of his brother George, the band that had robbed the Liberty bank back in 1866 became the James-Younger gang. The band was only loosely organized, and different men rode along in almost every raid (usually Cole Younger's brothers, the James boys' relatives, and old bushwhackers), but now Cole Younger and Jesse and Frank James formed the core of the group. Over time, young Jesse— with his cool nerves, almost reckless courage, and forceful presence—emerged as the leader, and the band would often be called simply the James gang.

In the meantime, however, the bandits dispersed and tried to stay out of sight until Bligh's investigation grew cold. Local people knew the James boys as well-armed, tough young men, but the authorities did not suspect them in any of the robberies over the last few years as Bligh had not yet made his findings public. For almost two years, nothing was heard from them.

At the end of 1869, however, Jesse and Frank James planned another robbery, much closer to home than Kentucky. On December 7, 1869, two men rode into Gallatin, northeast of Clay County, and dismounted their horses in front of the Daviess County Savings Bank. One of the men, probably Frank, walked up to the counter and asked Captain John Sheets, the owner of the bank, for change for a $100 bill. Sheets went to get the money out of the safe when Jesse approached him and said he would change the bill if Sheets wrote out a receipt. As Sheets started writing the receipt Jesse drew his revolver and shot him twice, in the head and chest. The bandits then opened fire on William McDowell, the bank clerk. McDowell was hit in the arm, but he made it outside and raised the alarm.

Jesse and Frank quickly stuffed several hundred dollars into their grain sack and ran to their horses. As the townspeople scrambled out to find out what was going on, Jesse's horse went wild, throwing him off the saddle and dragging him by the foot for several yards before he could pull free of the tangled stirrup. Frank waited as Jesse jumped up on the back of his horse, and then the two brothers galloped out of town, leaving Jesse's mount behind. Once they had cleared Gallatin, they stole a farmer's horse for Jesse. They hid out in the woods during the day, and then kidnapped a local man that night to guide them through the countryside in order to avoid the town of Kidder.

The seemingly senseless shooting raised a storm of anger and confusion. The bank clerk told reporters that the gunman had cursed as he shot Sheets, saying that Sheets and "Cox" had caused the death of his "brother" and that he wanted revenge. The man who had been kidnapped as a guide also said that the outlaws had declared Sheets's death revenge for the death of a brother.

It turned out that Sheets had fought in the battle where Major S. P. Cox's Union troops had killed Bloody Bill Anderson. It was known that Jesse had sworn revenge on the killers of his old commander (whom he certainly considered a "brother"), and the clerk reported that the gunman clearly recognized Sheets when he fired. The final evidence linking Jesse to the crime was the horse the outlaws had left behind. The Daviess County sheriff discovered that the unusually fine, fast horse abandoned by the killer belonged to Jesse James of Clay County.

The murder of Captain Sheets sparked a huge manhunt. Sheets's widow and the businesses of Gallatin offered a $3,000 reward for the capture of the murderer. The governor, Joseph McClurg, ordered the local militia to help catch or kill the bandits. After Jesse's horse was identified, Daviess County deputy sheriff John Thomason, his son Oscar, and two other men from Gallatin loaded their rifles and revolvers and set out for Clay County. There they carefully surrounded the Samuel house as Thomason and his son went to the front door. But the James boys knew

This display of the well-used paraphernalia of the James gang includes several guns and the boots Jesse was wearing when he died.

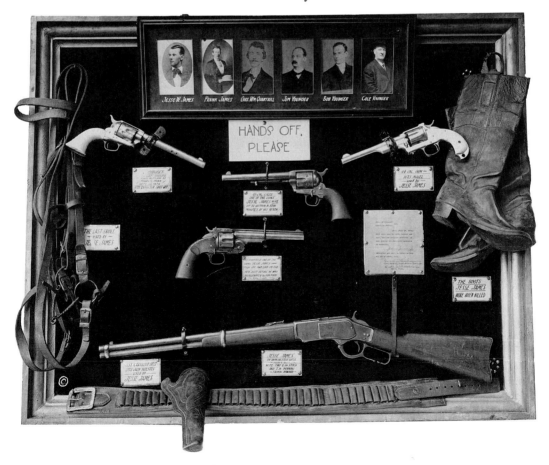

about the raid ahead of time. Before Thomason could knock, a young black child ran out the door and down to the stable. He opened the stable door and out sprinted two horses carrying Frank and Jesse.

The two men jumped their horses over the barnyard fence as they exchanged fire with the four men from Gallatin. The Daviess County posse tried to pursue, but only Thomason's horse cleared the fence. During a running gunfight on horseback, Thomason's horse went wild, sprinting out of control until he actually caught up with the James brothers. As the three raced along neck and neck, Jesse James calmly aimed his revolver and squeezed the trigger. Thomason's horse fell dead, leaving the deputy sheriff stranded as the outlaws escaped.

For the first time in the long string of bank robberies, Jesse and Frank James were publicly denounced by the authorities as criminals. The ruthless murder of Captain Sheets and their spectacular escape had turned them into celebrities almost overnight. But the biggest boost to their fame came from an old friend and newspaperman, Major John Newman Edwards.

Both of the James boys had met and befriended Edwards during the Civil War, when he was General Joseph Shelby's adjutant. When Edwards returned to Missouri after the war, he helped found the *Kansas City Times*. Edwards had stayed in touch with the brothers, and when they fell under suspicion he defended them in the *Times*—turning them into folk heroes in the process.

After the authorities in Gallatin accused Jesse and Frank James of the crime, Edwards printed a letter that he claimed had been written by Jesse. In the letter, Jesse said he was innocent, arguing that he could never get a fair trial in Radical-ruled Missouri. "It is true that during the war I was a Confederate soldier," the letter said, "and fought under the black flag, but since then I have lived as a peaceable citizen, and obeyed the laws of the United States to the best of my knowledge."

John Edwards, not Jesse James, probably wrote the letter. (Edwards often wrote books and letters for friends; his works included, for instance, Shelby's memoirs.) It began a long series of letters over the years, written in Jesse's name, which appeared in the press (and always in newspapers edited by John Newman Edwards) immediately after the authorities blamed a crime on the James brothers. These letters, and the editorials about Jesse that Edwards often wrote, claimed that Jesse and Frank had become outlaws because of the wrongs they had suffered during the war and under the Republican government. Even as Edwards wrote that the James boys were innocent, he praised their bravery and skill with the horse and revolver.

From then on, Edwards acted as a publicist for Jesse James. He carefully built a new public image for the man who had once been a teenage killer among a band of fanatical murderers. In Edwards's newspapers, Jesse James became the avenger of the lost cause of the Confederacy, striking back at the rich and corrupt Republican politicians and businessmen. In his obituary of Jesse, Edwards summed up his views with one angry sentence: "Would to God he were alive today to make a righteous butchery of a few more of them."

With the help of newspaperman John Newman Edwards, Jesse James spruced up his image and became a folk hero.

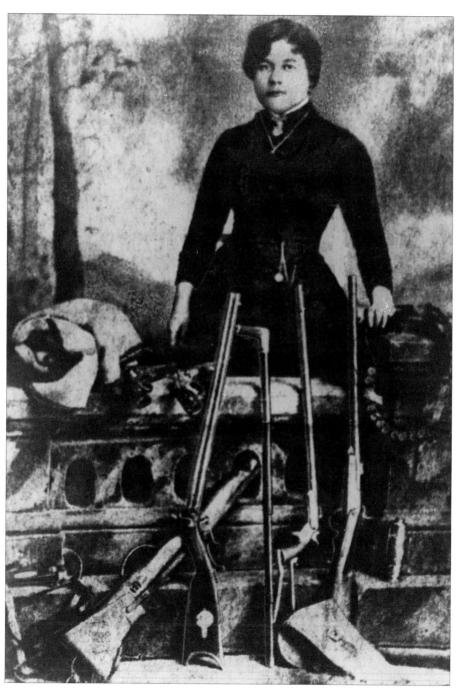

Jesse James's wife, Zerelda "Zee" James—who was also his first cousin—
poses with a few of her husband's weapons shortly after his death.

7

Politics and Pinkertons

EVERY NEWSPAPER IN THE STATE carried the dramatic story of the Gallatin holdup, Sheets's murder, and the James brothers' spectacular escape from the Daviess County posse. With all the publicity, the boys stayed at the safest hideout they could find: their mother and stepfather's farm in Clay County.

In Clay County the two brothers could relax; they knew most of the people who lived in the county, and they were related to many of them. The people of Clay County did not need Edwards to tell them that the James boys were heroes; Clay had been a hotbed of bushwhacker activity during the war, and the people hated the Radical Republican government running the state. They did not mind that Jesse and Frank made a nice profit while they robbed—the people of Clay would never turn them in.

After the Gallatin manhunt ran out of steam, the brothers recruited a local boy from Kearney, Clell Miller, to ride with them on another bank raid. On June 3, 1871, Jesse, Frank, Cole Younger, and Clell

Miller rode north into Iowa, to the town of Corydon. The streets were empty; almost all of the locals had crowded into the church to listen to a noted politician deliver a speech. The bandits quickly robbed the bank and then rode to the church to join the meeting. Seeing the chance to have a little fun, Jesse interrupted to inform everyone that the bank had just been robbed. The people in the crowd shouted at him to quiet down so the speaker could continue. By the time someone thought to check the bank, the four had already started back to Missouri with about $6,000. Once again, John Edwards's newspaper published a letter, supposedly from Jesse James, proclaiming Jesse's innocence.

After laying low for almost a year, working peacefully on their families' farms, Cole and the James boys rode into Columbia, Kentucky, in early 1872, pretending to be cattle buyers as they scouted out the local bank. While they prepared for the robbery, they stayed at the home of a wealthy farmer. Much to Frank James's delight, the farmer owned a copy of *The Pilgrim's Progress*. Frank had almost finished reading the book when the boys robbed the Columbia Deposit Bank on April 29, 1872, and rode back to Missouri.

The robbery in Kentucky, however, had not taken in much money. Jesse James and Cole Younger agreed on another holdup as the summer drew to a close. But instead of going after another bank, Jesse suggested their boldest act yet: to rob the front gate of the Kansas City Fair, an event attended by thousands of people each day. Frank backed out, but Cole and John Younger agreed to take part. On September 26, 1872, the 3 men rode through a huge crowd of almost 10,000 people in broad daylight and seized the metal box containing the admission fees. The cashier fought back, and a stray bullet struck a little girl in the leg as the three broke free and made off with almost a thousand dollars. The next day, John Edwards published an editorial regretting the girl's injury but praising the bandits for their bravery.

Once again, Edwards published a letter that allegedly came from the bandits. This letter, however, did not protest innocence. Instead, it described the holdup as an act of resistance against the Republicans running the state and the country. Armed robbery, it said, was nothing compared to the corruption of President Grant's Republican administration in Washington. The bandits only killed in self-defense, the letter went on, saying, "We rob the rich and give it to the poor."

The letter reflected Edwards's sure sense of the changes in Missouri politics. It was a time known as the Gilded Age, when railroads and wealthy speculators made millions while small farmers sank deep into debt. The people of western Missouri, still struggling to recover from the devastation of the Civil War, hated the government and despised the scandals among President Grant's advisers (including an outrageous attempt to corner the gold market in 1869).

The era of Reconstruction saw great advances in industrialization and civil rights: new railroads came to poor and isolated parts of the country, including Missouri, and black Americans won full citizenship and the right to vote with the Civil Rights Act of 1866 and the 13th, 14th, and 15th Amendments to the Constitution. Civil rights laws, however, meant little to the farmers of the Border who had fought for the Confederacy and slavery. They hated the Republicans, and all the banks, railroad companies, and businessmen who racked up profits while Republicans ran the state.

But the Southerners in Missouri were soon to have political revenge. In 1870, the voters repealed the oath of loyalty in a referendum; they also voted down the Republican candidate for governor. The Democrats won four congressional seats and a majority in the lower house of the General Assembly (the state legislature). The days when Radical Republicans occupied almost every public office, when lynch mobs could attack former Confederates while the sheriff looked the other way, were over.

The gang knew that public opinion was turning in their favor. On May 27, 1873, they struck a bank in Ste. Genevieve, Missouri, shouting "Hurrah for Hildebrand!" (the name of a local guerrilla hero noted for his savagery against German immigrants during the war) as they rode through the streets with $4,000 in their grain sack. Then, on July 21, 1873, they went after the most hated institution of all: the railroads.

During the years of Radical rule, Missouri's county governments had issued more than $18 million worth of bonds to finance the expanding railroads. In many places, the people voted against issuing the bonds, but often the county judges (who were usually Republicans) issued them anyway. Between 1865 and 1870 the railroad companies almost doubled the total miles of track in the state. With each year they grew more powerful, buying up land and setting high rates for shipping goods. Local farmers, deep in debt from buying new farm machinery after the Civil War, could barely afford to send their crops, hogs, and cattle by train. Meanwhile, the counties raised taxes drastically to pay the interest on the railway bonds.

The people who had driven out the Indians and the Mormons, invaded abolitionist Kansas, and fought a guerrilla war against the Union army now attacked their own county governments for taxing them to aid the railroads. In 1869, a mob in Knox County threatened to lynch the local judges. In Cass County, local men formed a secret association to encourage people not to pay their taxes. In 1872, three Cass officials got caught in a conspiracy to give even more money to the railroads. As they tried to escape to Kansas City, a crowd dressed in Ku Klux Klan robes stopped their train, hauled them off, and riddled their bodies with scores of bullets. As the taxpayer revolt spread across Missouri, the people fastened their hatred on the railroad companies and their government friends.

It was no coincidence, then, when the James and Younger brothers decided to rob the Chicago, Rock Island,

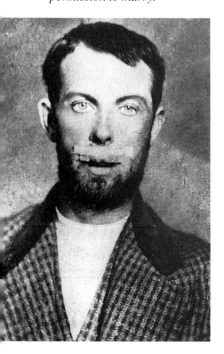

Gang member Jim Younger was captured after the James gang's failed robbery attempt in Northfield, Minnesota, in 1876. This picture was taken at the time of his trial (note the bandage on his upper lip where he was struck by a bullet in the mayhem). After his release from prison in 1902, Jim Younger committed suicide when the parole authorities denied him permission to marry.

and Pacific Railroad in July 1873. They had learned that a train carrying a large shipment of gold would pass through Council Bluffs, Iowa. Jesse and Frank James, Cole Younger, and three or four others (probably including some of Cole's brothers) rode north to Council Bluffs, and met on the evening of July 21 at a blind curve in the tracks outside of town. As the train approached, they pulled a rail out of line, sending the engine toppling over and killing the engineer, John Rafferty. Pulling on Ku Klux Klan masks (Klansmen were heroes to white Southerners), they entered the train and discovered they had missed the gold shipment by a matter of hours. Instead, they had to be happy with $2,000 from the safe in the express delivery company's car and what they could collect from the passengers. Jesse calmly directed the entire robbery, down to a cheerful wave to the passengers as the gang rode away.

The spectacular holdup caused a national sensation. The authorities and newspapers assumed that the James boys had pulled it off—and more than a few people were happy to see them do it. The railroad companies, however, took the robbery very seriously. Immediately after the James-Younger gang struck, several of them agreed to cooperate to destroy this new threat. Rather than rely on local sheriffs and posses, they called in the best lawmen in the country: the Pinkerton National Detective Agency.

The Pinkertons, as the detectives were known, had become famous by spying for the Union army during the war (when the agency was called the Pinkerton Government Guard). Now Allan Pinkerton and his sons and employees searched for criminals across the country. The Pinkertons had been called in once before on the James boys, after the Corydon robbery, when Robert Pinkerton had followed the gang's trail back to Missouri before losing them. In August 1873, some of the top men from the agency's Chicago office traveled to Iowa to lead the latest search, along with an Iowa sheriff and some men from Missouri.

Allan Pinkerton, shown here on horseback, spent years tracking Jesse James, who successfully eluded him throughout his career.

The group soon found the trail of the James boys, even catching a horse that Jesse had lost. The Pinkertons learned that the boys had ridden to Johnson City, in St. Clair County, to meet at the home of the Youngers. The Missouri, Kansas, and Texas Railroad company provided a special train to take the detectives to Johnson City, but by the time they surrounded the Youngers' house the gang had escaped.

The repeated failure to capture the bandits infuriated the new governor, Silas Woodson. In October 1873, he offered a $2,000 reward for "the bodies of said Frank and Jesse James." The James brothers, however, remained perfectly safe. Not even the $2,000 bounty could shake the loyalty of Clay County.

Neither the Pinkertons nor the governor's offer slowed down the gang's activities. In January 1874, they appeared in Hot Springs, Arkansas, where they stopped a stagecoach full of wealthy passengers. Once again the gang played the roles of Southern heroes. Cole Younger announced that they would not rob Confederate veterans, graciously returning a watch and some money to a man who had been in the Southern army.

Two weeks later, on the afternoon of January 31, 1874, the James and Younger brothers rode up to a flag station for the Iron Mountain railroad at Gad's Hill, about 100 miles north of St. Louis. After taking the signalmen at Gad's Hill prisoner, they put a red flag on the track to stop a train headed for Little Rock. With guns drawn, they boarded the train and set to work robbing the passengers and the safe.

By now the outlaws openly imitated Robin Hood. As they walked up the aisles of the passenger cars, they carefully checked for calluses on the hands of the men on the train to see if they were laborers. They did not want to take the money of workingmen, the bandits announced, they only wanted to rob the rich "plug hat gentlemen." They even acted as their own press agents, handing the crew a prepared account of the robbery with a blank space to be filled in with the amount of the loot. After the holdup, word went out that the bandits had stayed at the homes of farmers during their escape across Missouri, acting like respectful guests and paying well for their bed and board.

After Gad's Hill, however, the Pinkertons took up the case again. On March 10, 1874, a young detective named John Whicher arrived in Liberty. He told the president of

After a sensational robbery in July 1873, in which the James gang derailed a train, toppling it and killing the conductor, the railroads pooled forces to combat the outlaws. They hired the Pinkerton detectives and offered a large reward for the capture of the bandits.

the commercial bank in town and a former sheriff that he planned to go in disguise to the Samuel farm and get work as a farmhand. He would then bide his time until he could capture the James boys and bring them in. The former sheriff warned Whicher that it was a foolish idea, saying that Zerelda Samuel posed as dangerous a threat as her sons. Whicher ignored the warning and took a train to Kearney, where he started hiking up the road to the Samuel place.

John Whicher probably never reached the home of Jesse and Frank James. Before he even got off the train in Kearney, the sheriff of Clay County, George E. Patton, learned of his mission and rode out to pay a visit to his old friends, the James brothers. That night, a local ferryman took Jesse James, Arthur McCoy, Bloody Bill Anderson's brother Jim, and a bound and gagged prisoner across the Missouri River to Jackson County at three in the morning. With a straight face, Jesse told the ferry pilot that they were lawmen guarding a dangerous outlaw. Whicher's body turned up the next day along a road in Jackson County, shot through the head and chest.

A few days later, two other Pinkertons went with a former deputy sheriff to try and round up the Younger brothers near Johnson City. A roadside gunfight on horseback between the posse and Jim and John Younger left one Pinkerton, the former deputy, and John Younger dead. Jim survived, and the second Pinkerton (John Boyle, from St. Louis) escaped unharmed.

Barely a month later, on April 24, 1874, the extended James and Samuel family gathered at the home of Zee Mimms's sister for a special ceremony. With a Methodist minister, an uncle, presiding, Jesse finally married his cousin after being engaged for nine years. According to legend, Jesse had to convince Reverend William James of his innocence in the famous robberies before the minister would marry them. In June, the newspapers in St. Louis and elsewhere learned the news and published stories about the wedding. By then, however, the couple had gone to Sherman, Texas, for their honeymoon. There Jesse amused himself with a few stagecoach robberies. The couple returned to Missouri by August, settling in Kansas City.

On August 30, 1874, Jesse and Cole Younger each took a few men and simultaneously held up coaches 25 miles apart near the Missouri River. They carried out the robberies in broad daylight, in view of dozens of people on both sides of the river. The bandits did no harm to their victims (in fact, a professor who was on the coach told a reporter that "he was exceedingly glad, as he had to be robbed, that it was done by first class artists, by men of national reputation"), but the robberies caused a state-wide scandal.

In fact, Jesse James's dramatic robberies in 1873 and 1874 made him and his gang the focus of a huge battle for the future of Missouri. An election was approaching at the end of 1874, and no issue seemed more important to the public than the capture—or the alleged heroism—of the outlaws. It marked the start of a year that would take Jesse James from the edge of destruction to the height of popularity—and then back to the edge once more.

In this illustration from a boys' adventure magazine, Jesse James flags down an oncoming train. In January 1874, the James gang robbed a train in Missouri using a similar tactic.

"Halt sir; stand and deliver!" demands Jesse James in this picture from a 1900 boys' adventure magazine. A victim of one of the gang's stage-coach hold-ups in 1874 told a reporter afterward that "he was exceedingly glad, as he had to be robbed, that it was done by first class artists, by men of national reputation."

8

The Year of the
James Gang

"THE BANDIT STATE OF MISSOURI," the Eastern newspapers called it by 1874. When the James-Younger gang went from local heroes to national celebrities, they created the impression that Missouri sheltered a beehive of murdering robbers. People outside the state found it impossible to believe that well-known bandits could walk free in Missouri year after year. The *Chicago Tribune* called the failure to capture the James boys "a disgrace." The *New York Herald* said it was "due to the unpardonable cowardice of the whole community."

Of all the issues at stake in the election of 1874, none got more attention than the James gang. Three parties nominated candidates for governor: the Democrats, the Republicans, and the new People's party. The Republicans cooperated with the new party to try to defeat the Democrats, and the two groups denounced the Democratic governor and legislature again and again for failing to break up the James-Younger gang. Missouri's image as the "bandit state," they argued, scared off immigrants and investors.

Democratic governor Silas Woodson did his best to bring the bandits in, but he faced a difficult task. Not only did the people of Clay and other counties protect the James and Younger boys, but the authorities possessed no reliable descriptions, let alone photographs, of the bandits. The gang itself changed from one robbery to the next. The leaders remained the James brothers and Cole Younger, but the other men came from a network of former bushwhackers, relatives, and local desperadoes such as Cole's brothers Jim and Bob, and the James boys' many cousins and in-laws. And the gang usually pulled only two or three holdups a year, leaving plenty of the time for the bandits to scatter and the trail to grow cold. With the election coming up, Governor Woodson decided the time had come for extreme measures.

In a special address to the General Assembly, Woodson denounced the bandits as a continuing humiliation for the state of Missouri. They had to be stopped, he said, and he asked for $10,000 to hire a force of secret agents to track the gang down. He also requested a special bill to reactivate the militia to capture the James and Younger brothers. The assembly quickly approved the special fund.

The governor, however, won only half a success. Many of the Democratic legislators were ex-Confederates who sympathized with the bandits; more than one-third of the members of the lower house of the assembly refused to vote on the secret agent fund. They also managed to kill off the militia bill and to block a resolution that singled out the James and Younger brothers as outlaws.

Frank and Jesse benefited from a little campaigning from their mother, Zerelda Samuel. In October, she visited the editor of the *Caucasian*, an anti-Republican newspaper in Lexington. The paper described her as a "tall, dignified lady, of about forty-eight years; graceful in carriage and gesture; calm and quiet in demeanor, with a ripple of fire now and then breaking through the placid surface; and of far more than ordinary intelligence and culture." Playing her role like a talented actress, Zerelda described the suffering the family had endured since before the Civil War and claimed that her sons lived in Mexico while other men committed these notorious crimes. No mother, she said, ever had finer sons than Frank and Jesse.

Zerelda's visit to the newspaper was part of a plan by the gang to confuse the authorities and create doubt about their guilt. With the help of John Newman Edwards, the boys had carefully polished their images as Robin Hood–style outlaws; now they sowed confusion with equal care. In November, a newspaper edited by a brother-in-law of the Youngers' published a letter from Cole, in which he said he hated Jesse James and had not spoken to him for years.

In December, the James and Younger brothers rode to Muncie, Kansas (not far from Kansas City), where they held up a train on the Kansas Pacific Railroad. They rode off with $30,000, though a friend of Frank and Jesse's who had taken part in the robbery was later caught and killed as he tried to escape from jail. But most important of all, the Pinkertons had returned.

Sometime toward the end of 1874, the Pinkertons (as always, hired by the railroads) started a new scheme to track down and capture the James boys. Two detectives named George Warren and J. W. Ragsdale sent special agent Jack Ladd to find work on a farm close to the Samuel place.

Ladd was smarter than the reckless John Whicher. He got a job on Daniel Askew's farm, right next door to the

This house in Kearney, Missouri, served as a refuge for Frank and Jesse James throughout their outlaw careers. The Samuel farm, home of their mother, Zerelda, and their stepfather, Reuben Samuel, was a dangerous place to venture for those not friendly with the outlaws' numerous friends and relatives in Clay County.

Jesse James's stoic mother, Zerelda Samuel, lost part of her right arm in the explosion caused by the Pinkerton detectives during an attempted raid on the night of January 26, 1875.

Samuel farm. As he worked he kept a low profile and spied on the Samuel family without arousing any suspicion. A lawyer in Liberty, Samuel Hardwicke, acted as the messenger for Ladd, passing along his information through coded telegrams to another Pinkerton agent. In late January 1875, Ladd sent word to Warren and Ragsdale, through one of Hardwicke's coded telegrams, that the James brothers had returned home. The Pinkertons and the railroad companies had prepared for this moment for months, keeping their plan secret even from the governor. On January 26, 1875, they went into action.

That night a special train, run by William Westfall, pulled to a stop outside of Kearney. Several Pinkerton detectives got off, unloaded their horses, and rode to meet with Jack Ladd. As they rode through the dark, they carried two unusually heavy bundles—the products of a special order made by a workshop in St. Louis or Chicago. Guided by Ladd, they quietly surrounded the Samuel house deep in the middle of the night.

The next thing Zerelda and her husband knew, a heavy sound came from the kitchen. When they and their children ran to investigate, they saw a flaming ball of cotton on the floor, soaked with kerosene. Another blazing bundle came crashing through a window as they watched. Dr. Samuel ran to get a poker and a shovel; as he pushed the flaming items toward the fireplace, he realized that a heavy metal ball was at the center of each. Then, as the burning cotton and metal spheres rolled into the hearth, they exploded. Jagged fragments of metal flew out, killing Jesse's nine-year-old half brother Archie Samuel. Another piece badly damaged Zerelda's right hand. One of the family's black servants in the room also suffered a light wound.

Immediately after the explosion James Hall, a young neighbor from the farm south of the Samuels' who had seen what had happened, rode off to Kearney and brought back Dr. James Scruggs. Dr. Scruggs told Zerelda that her hand would have to be amputated. She ordered everyone out of the room. Once she was alone, Jesse James emerged from hiding to say good-bye. Sneaking out the back, he took Dr. Scruggs's horse and galloped off to escape.

The Pinkertons had scrambled off when the iron balls exploded. They had intended only to start a fire with the devices, in order to force the family (and Jesse) to leave the house; instead, the coals in the fireplace had overheated them, causing them to explode. Surprised and alarmed, they abandoned the plan and rode back to meet William Westfall's special train without anything to show for the expedition.

One of the detectives, however, had lost his revolver outside the Samuel house as he ran off in panic. The next day it was found, stamped with "P.G.G."—the initials of the Pinkerton Government Guard, the Civil War name for the agency. The Democrats held up the revolver as proof that the Pinkertons and railroad companies had carried out the attack. Every newspaper in the state condemned the raid. The *Kansas City Times* wrote that "there is no crime, however dastardly, which merits a retribution as savage and fiendish as the one which these men acting under the semblance of law have perpetrated."

Outrage swept the state of Missouri. The General Assembly passed a resolution demanding that Governor Hardin investigate the bombing. The Republicans fought back in favor of the railroads, offering a resolution calling for an investigation of the James brothers, but the legislature voted it down. In March a grand jury in Clay County began investigating the event, hearing testimony from everyone from Dr. Scruggs to former governor Silas Woodson. Even Samuel Hardwicke, the go-between for the Pinkertons, testified about his role. In the end, the grand jury indicted Jack Ladd, Robert King, and Allan Pinkerton himself for the murder of Archie Samuel.

The bomb attack built up tremendous sympathy for the James and Younger brothers. On March 8, 1875, the *St. Louis Dispatch* published an open plea for amnesty for the gang, and other papers echoed the call. On March 17, the General Assembly introduced a resolution that offered amnesty for their actions during the war, promising a fair trial for any crimes committed since 1865.

The resolution, written in flowery language, called the bandits "too brave to be mean; too generous to be revengeful, and too gallant and honorable to betray a friend or break a promise." In fact, it probably came from the pen of none other than Major John Newman Edwards. In the end, the General Assembly voted on a resolution that left out the lavish praise of the outlaws. This new version won more than half of the vote but failed to pass with the required two-thirds majority.

Meanwhile, Jesse and Frank took revenge on their enemies. Jack Ladd disappeared and was believed to have been killed the night of the attack. Next came Daniel Askew. On April 12, 1875, Askew answered a knock in the middle of the night. When he opened the door someone shot him dead. The brothers and their friends also threatened other local men they suspected of helping the Pinkertons. Samuel Hardwicke, convinced that he would be killed, fled to Minnesota.

Sheriff John Groom wrote to Governor Hardin that the fear that gripped Clay County was as bad "as at any time during the war." In the aftermath of the bombing of the Samuel farm and the murders of Ladd and Askew, everyone in Clay County who did not think of the James boys as heroes grew too frightened to speak out against them.

As the General Assembly and the local grand jury looked into the Pinkerton raid, Jesse and Frank James laid low, waiting for the furor to pass. Frank had eloped with Annie Ralston, a woman from Jackson County, to Omaha in 1874, and he probably spent most of 1875 living with her in Nebraska. Jesse continued to live quietly in Kansas City with Zee, and on December 31, 1875, she gave birth to their first child, a boy they named Jesse Edwards—very likely in honor of John Newman Edwards.

Eight-year-old Archie Samuel, half brother of Frank and Jesse James, was killed when a burning flare thrown in the window of the Samuels' home by the Pinkerton detectives exploded after it was shoved into the fireplace.

In the summer of 1876 the Jameses reunited with the Youngers for another big job. Once again, they selected a train as their target. Since the gang's war with the railroads had begun, they had robbed more and more trains, and fewer banks. This time the James brothers and Cole Younger were joined by Cole's brother Bob, Clell Miller, and two other local desperadoes, Hobbs Kerry and Samuel Wells. An outlaw from Minnesota named William Stiles (who went by the name of Bill Chadwell), rode along as well.

On the evening of July 7, 1876, the gang flagged down a train on the Missouri Pacific Railroad at a bridge at Rocky Cut, not far from Otterville, Missouri. As the passengers sang hymns under the guidance of a minister and the guns of an outlaw guard, the gang looted the express safes of more than $15,000. They divided the loot and split up. But after the robbery, the chief of the St. Louis police caught Hobbs Kerry in southwestern Missouri. Kerry, who had never committed a crime before, confessed and named the others.

Zerelda Samuel again denied that her sons were guilty, and another letter allegedly from Jesse appeared in the *Kansas City Times*. The newspaper itself complained about the way the big city detectives had come into western Missouri to arrest local men. The Pinkertons, however, believed the James and Younger brothers had robbed the train at Rocky Cut. On August 11, 1876, thinking they would find Frank hiding with his in-laws, they raided the home of Annie Ralston's parents. The Ralstons, however, had no idea where their daughter was, let alone Frank and Jesse James. The detectives returned to their offices empty-handed. Once again they had lost the trail of the bandits. Then, on September 7, 1876, word came from Northfield, Minnesota, that the gang had been found and defeated at last.

The children of Jesse and Zee James, Mary and Jesse Edwards. The younger Jesse grew up to become a lawyer.

9

Betrayal

IN THE LATE SUMMER or early autumn of 1876, J. D. Howard and B. J. Woodson moved with their wives to the outskirts of Nashville, Tennessee. Woodson, a dignified man in his early thirties, went on to lead a quiet life in the town of Eaton Creek, working hard at farming and other jobs. His family thrived in Tennessee, and on February 6, 1878, his wife Fannie Woodson gave birth to a boy. Drawing on names from family tradition, the couple named the baby Robert Franklin.

Woodson's friend, J. D. Howard, also led a calm existence with his wife, Josie, and his young son, though he did not work quite as hard as Woodson. A tall, restless, bearded man with striking blue eyes, he attended the local church, farmed, tried his hand as a wheat merchant, and showed a taste for gambling. Josie Howard had twins who died soon after birth, and she suffered from illness herself. On July 17, 1879, however, Mrs. Howard gave birth to a healthy girl they named Mary.

None of the neighbors had any reason to suspect that Woodson and Howard were, in fact, Frank and Jesse James. After they escaped the

Jesse James lived much of his life under the alias J. D. Howard, and he often wore a full beard, perhaps to mask his identity.

manhunt that followed the Northfield disaster and recuperated from their wounds, not even Clay County or the familiar streets of Kansas City seemed safe to the two outlaws. But in the area around Nashville, they spent the next three years living peacefully. Frank James seemed to enjoy his new life, but Jesse grew restless. In mid-1879, Jesse began to disappear from Nashville for weeks at a time as he paid visits to certain male relatives and old friends.

The world had almost begun to think it had seen the last of Jesse James when, after an absence of three years, he struck again. On the night of October 8, 1879, he led a new gang of five men to the town of Glendale, in Jackson County, Missouri. There they flagged down a train on the Chicago and Alton Railroad and took $6,000 from the express car safe.

The men who rode with Jesse James to Glendale were all new to the gang. His cousin Wood Hite, an old companion from Bloody Bill Anderson's guerrillas, took part, as did Ed Miller, brother of the late Clell Miller, and Bill Ryan, another old bushwhacker. Ryan brought along an inexperienced man named Tucker Bassham. Dick Liddil rounded out the group; Frank James had declined to take part and stayed behind in Tennessee.

The news of the robbery snapped Jesse James back into the headlines—and an even more dramatic story about the outlaw soon followed. Jesse James, the papers reported in November 1879, had died at the hands of George Shepherd. Shepherd, who had finally been released from the Kentucky prison after serving time for the Russellville robbery, announced that he had plotted with Marshal James Ligget to round up the James gang. One day, he said, as he rode alongside Jesse, he had surprised the famous bandit and shot him in the head.

Robert Pinkerton, for one, did not believe the story. "No one should know more about Jesse James than I do," he said, "for our men have chased him from one end of the country to the other. His gang killed two of our detectives . . . and I consider Jesse James the worst man, without exception, in America. He is utterly devoid of fear." Pinkerton went on, "I don't believe Shepherd would dare shoot at him." Before long, the world would know that Robert Pinkerton was right: Jesse James still lived.

Meanwhile, another election approached and the outlaws once again rose to the center of the 1880 campaign. The Republicans passed a platform that denounced the Democrats for failing to capture the James brothers. The gang, the Republicans claimed, "prevented immigration into the State and the introduction of capital and the growth and development of industries."

The Republicans did not stand alone in their claim that the bandits had harmed Missouri. The *New York Illustrated News* later said the damage "inflicted upon Missouri [by the James gang] is beyond calculation. . . . No man ventured within its borders unless the stern necessities of business compelled him; when a traveler got into a Missouri train he did so with the same feeling that a man has when going into battle—with little expectation of getting through alive."

The Democrats rose to the challenge. They nominated Thomas T. Crittenden for governor. Crittenden had fought for the Union during the war, and he had taken a leading part in rebuilding the party during Reconstruction. Now he allied himself closely with the railroad and rail express delivery companies, and he resolved to destroy the outlaws with more determination than any Democrat had in the last 10 years.

In the 1880 election, the people of Missouri showed how much things had changed since the 1860s and early 1870s, when many of them had considered the James brothers heroes. Crittenden won the election for governor, and William H. Wallace was elected public prosecutor in Jackson County, where the gang had long found strong support. Western Missouri was no longer the Border, violent, angry, and torn by war; now it was a prospering, well-developed area where many people had grown tired of the banditry. Wallace openly denounced Jesse and Frank

James, despite the death threats he received from former bushwhackers. Governor Crittenden set the new tone when he announced in his inaugural address, "We should let all know that Missouri cannot be the home and abiding place of lawlessness of any character."

The pressure on Jesse James began to build almost immediately. After the Glendale robbery, he took Bill Ryan (who lived nearby) to rob a tourist coach at Mammoth Cave in Kentucky, in late 1880. Then in March 1881, he talked Frank into joining him in his renewed career in crime. Along with Bill Ryan, the two brothers held up a government paymaster in Muscle Shoals, Alabama. But at the end of the month, everything went sour. Bill Ryan got drunk at a local tavern and loudly proclaimed his identity as a feared outlaw. The local authorities promptly arrested him and sent him back to Missouri to stand trial for the Glendale robbery.

After Ryan's arrest, Jesse James quickly packed up his wife and two children and moved away from Nashville. After a brief stay with his cousins Wood and Clarence Hite in Kentucky, he returned to Kansas City. Despite the determination of the governor and the Jackson County prosecutor to capture him, he still trusted in his popular support in Missouri, his knowledge of the countryside, and the fact that the police had no reliable description of his physical appearance.

In the summer of 1881 he struck again. On the night of July 15, Jesse and Frank James and three others boarded a train headed east from Kansas City on the Rock Island Railroad. The other men were Wood Hite, Clarence Hite, and Dick Liddil. But Jesse had more in mind than robbing the express safe. After boarding, he calmly waited with Frank in the last car as the conductor entered, collecting tickets. Jesse knew the conductor to be William Westfall—the man who had run the train that carried the Pinkertons to Kearney in 1875, the night the Samuel home was bombed. As Westfall walked by, Jesse stood and shot him in the back. As the passengers panicked, Frank shot and killed a stone mason named Frank McMillan. After forcing the train to a halt near the town of Winston, they emptied the express safe of $8,000 to $10,000 in gold and cash and escaped into the night.

The Winston holdup humiliated the new governor. Newspapers as far away as Massachusetts mocked Missouri. St. Louis's rival city, Chicago, was especially harsh; the *Chicago Times* called Missouri "the outlaw's paradise." Governor Crittenden was furious. Despite his determination to break up the gang, he suffered from the same handicaps that had foiled his predecessors. The people of western Missouri, he snorted, treated the James gang "like a pet band of outlaws." And state law hampered him further: the government could offer no more than $300 per outlaw as a reward—a small sum for the man Robert Pinkerton called "the worst man, without exception, in America." Instead, Crittenden decided to go to some friends outside of the government for help.

Immediately after the Winston robbery the governor called on an old associate, Colonel Wells H. Blodgett (an attorney for the Wabash Railroad), and asked him to arrange a meeting with the state's railroad executives. On July 27, 1881, the general managers of all the major railroad and express companies met with the governor in the Southern Hotel in St. Louis. At the end of the meeting, the businessmen pledged a total of $55,000 for the new reward fund. On July 28, 1881, officials began posting the notice: PROCLAMATION OF THE GOVERNOR OF MISSOURI! REWARDS FOR THE ARREST OF EXPRESS AND TRAIN ROBBERS. The governor offered $5,000 for each of the men involved in the Winston robbery, and $10,000 each for Frank and Jesse James. Someone in the gang, Crittenden thought, "would grow tired of the life, and more tired of being led on in blood and crime by a desperate leader."

Jesse James gave his answer on September 7, 1881. He had met with the gang at the farm of Charlie Ford, who was related by marriage to Jim Cummings (who often rode with the James gang). There he laid out plans for holding up a train known to be carrying $100,000—more money than they had ever taken before. On the night of the seventh at Blue Cut, just a few miles east of Independence, Jesse and Frank James, Dick Liddil, Clarence and Wood Hite, and Charlie Ford stopped a train on the Chicago and Alton Railroad. When they entered and opened the express safe, they found just a few thousand dollars. They had stopped the wrong train.

Jesse James flew into a rage. He smashed the express employee with the butt of his revolver until the man fell unconscious to the floor. Then the gang robbed the passengers, declaring that the robbery was an act of revenge against the Chicago and Alton Railroad for taking part in the reward offer. Once again, the outlaws escaped safely when their work was done.

The outlaws had embarrassed Governor Crittenden once again. The robbery came only a few weeks after the reward offer, and it took place only a few miles from Independence, where Bill Ryan was about to be tried for the Glendale holdup. Crittenden called vainly on the people of Missouri to "rise *en masse,*" to chase the bandits "by day or by night, until the entire band is either captured or exterminated."

In late September, William Wallace began the trial of Bill Ryan—and he introduced a surprise witness. Tucker Bassham, the illiterate man whom Ryan had brought along on the Glendale robbery, received a pardon from the governor in return for testifying. Tension hung over the trial that followed. Old Confederates packed the courthouse. They burned Bassham's home to the ground and threatened to kill Wallace and Bassham. Governor Crittenden even rushed to the scene with a shipment of weapons, in case of mass unrest. But in the end the jury convicted Ryan, and the judge sentenced him to 25 years in prison. Tucker Bassham quickly fled to another state.

Ryan's conviction marked a turning point for Jesse James. A member of Jesse's own gang had turned against him, and a jury from one of his old strongholds had convicted one of his gang. Even worse, a convention of former Confederate soldiers in Moberly, Missouri, passed a resolution supporting Crittenden's program for eliminating banditry.

Jesse James began to suspect his own men of plotting against him. He closely watched Ed Miller, who had saved about $600 from the recent robberies and was thinking about quitting. Jesse was convinced that he had turned traitor. One day that autumn, Jesse took Ed out in the country for a ride. Only Jesse came back. Later Charlie Ford asked where Miller was. Jesse, Ford reported, "said Miller was in bad health, and he did not think he could live long." Miller's body was found beside a country road with a bullet in the head.

As Jesse's fear of betrayal grew worse, he next suspected Jim Cummings. Cummings heard of Jesse's suspicions, and he fled the state in fear of his life. As the year passed, Jesse kept his revolvers on his body at all times. "He was so watchful," Charlie Ford said, "no man could get the drop on him." It was even said that he slept with his pistols in his hands.

On November 5, 1881, Jesse James moved out of Kansas City to St. Joseph, a prospering town of about 40,000 people, where he had found a house that offered better protection from a surprise attack. Known as the House on the Hill, it offered a commanding view of all approaches and provided numerous escape routes. In a stable attached to the house, he kept two horses, one always saddled and bridled, ready to be ridden on a moment's notice.

Even now, he made no attempt at disguise. He joined the local Presbyterian church and told his neighbors that he was a cattle buyer. Because a number of stock buyers (who would disappear for weeks at a time to look for animals to buy for St. Joseph's stockyards) lived in the area, people readily believed his story.

As autumn stretched into winter, Jesse James spent more of his time at Charlie Ford's place outside of Richmond, in Ray County. The ranks of his gang had grown

Charlie Ford, a member of Jesse James's gang, later turned against Jesse to obtain a reward.

thin, thanks to William Wallace and Jesse's own suspicions. Charlie's young brother Bob, however, eagerly
wanted to join; with so few men left, Jesse agreed to let
him in.

Bob Ford, however, had in mind the $10,000 reward.
His chance to collect the bounty came with a gunfight on
an early December morning. For some time, Dick Liddil
and Wood Hite had been rivals for Martha Bolton, the
Fords' widowed sister. This particular morning they both
showed up at her home. Tensions quickly rose, and they

began to quarrel over how the money from the Blue Cut robbery had been split up. In a moment they had their guns out, firing away. They only managed to wound one another until Bob Ford abruptly pulled his Smith and Wesson revolver and shot Wood Hite dead.

After killing Jesse James's cousin, Bob Ford explained the situation to Dick Liddil and his brother Charlie, who was also present. They were now enemies of Jesse and murderers before the law, Ford said. With Jesse, there would be no forgiveness. But with the law, Ford reasoned, they could make a deal—and share the reward money as well. Charlie and Dick Liddil agreed. In mid-December, they sent Martha Bolton on two important visits: one to Jackson County prosecutor William Wallace and a second to Governor Crittenden.

With a veil over her face, Bolton made Bob's proposal to the governor: Dick Liddil would surrender to the law and testify against the James gang—and, she hinted, Jesse James himself might be turned over to the law. In exchange, they wanted the reward money and freedom for Liddil. Crittenden told her to contact Clay County sheriff Timberlake and Kansas City police chief Craig. Bob Ford met with the lawmen and convinced them his offer was serious. Craig and Timberlake set up one more meeting.

At one o'clock on the morning of January 13, 1882, Governor Crittenden retired to his room after a fashionable annual ball at the St. James Hotel in Kansas City. Waiting for him was the young man with the Smith and Wesson. Crittenden and Bob Ford sealed the deal. Both men understood that Jesse would not be taken alive.

On January 24, Dick Liddil turned himself in to Sheriff Timberlake and immediately began to give him information. Less than a month later, Missouri lawmen arrested Jesse's cousin, Clarence Hite. Faced with Dick Liddil's testimony, Hite pleaded guilty to the charges of train robbery. At the end of March, the authorities announced that they had Dick Liddil in custody as well—though they kept secret the circumstances of his surrender.

*Bob Ford holds the gun he used
to kill Jesse James.*

Jesse James's world crumbled around him. First his cousin Wood had disappeared, then Dick Liddil vanished, and now Clarence had been arrested—and then pleaded guilty for no apparent reason. In just a few months, his gang had almost completely evaporated. Yet he continued to plan still another robbery, calling on Charlie Ford to help him scout out banks in the area. In the end, he decided to rob the bank in Platte City, Missouri, where a big murder trial due to start soon would draw attention away from the bank. Anxious about security after the recent arrests, he told the Ford brothers about a new precaution they would take to ensure his safety.

On March 31, 1882, Bob Ford called on Sheriff Timberlake to tell him that he would not see the sheriff for a few days. Jesse James had just asked Bob and Charlie Ford, the last two men left whom he trusted, to move in with him at his home in St. Joseph.

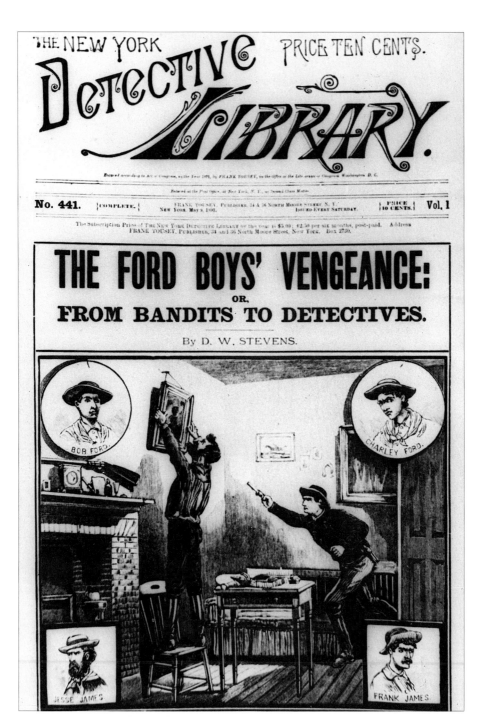

This cover of a dime novel from the New York Detective Library shows Bob Ford shooting Jesse James in the back of the head while Jesse stands on a chair to straighten a picture. The actual shooting on April 3, 1882, happened much the way it is portrayed here.

10

The Legend

DESPITE CONSTANT VIGILANCE, Bob and Charlie Ford could not get the drop on Jesse until the day he asked them to move in with him in St. Joseph. On the morning of April 3, 1882, as Zee worked in the kitchen, Bob Ford followed Jesse into another room, where Jesse stood up on a chair to dust a picture. For reasons that will never be known for certain, Jesse removed his revolvers and laid them on the bed before he climbed on the chair and turned his back to Ford. It has been suggested that James was concerned that he would look suspicious to anyone looking in the window, or that he wished to reassure the Ford brothers that he still trusted them after the surrender of Dick Liddil (so that he could shoot them later, out of sight of his pregnant wife). Some have even speculated that, with his gang in a shambles and the law closing in, Jesse was simply ready to die. Whatever the reason, it was a fateful decision. Bob Ford silently drew his pistol; when he cocked the hammer, Jesse turned his head to look, but before the outlaw could move, Ford fired a bullet into the back of his head. Zee raced into the room and screamed in horror as the Ford brothers ran from the house to report to the governor.

At a coroner's inquest after the murder, Zee James and Zerelda Samuel left no doubt that it was indeed Jesse who had been killed. Asked if the deceased was her son, Zerelda cried out, "Would to God that it were not!" She turned upon Dick Liddil, who was in the courtroom that day, and shouted, "Traitor! Traitor! Traitor!" Officials searched through Zee James's house and found many items that had been stolen over the years.

After the investigation, the authorities returned the body to Kearney by a special train. Hundreds of people attended the funeral; afterward the Samuel family buried Jesse in a plot on the farm where he was born.

In the wake of the killing, the St. Joseph lawmen arrested Bob and Charlie Ford and charged them with murder. They pleaded guilty, and the court sentenced them to

A crowd gathered around the house in St. Joseph, Missouri, after Jesse James was killed.

hang. Governor Crittenden, however, kept his half of the bargain. He pardoned the brothers and quietly paid out the reward money.

In the summer of 1882, John Newman Edwards opened secret negotiations with Governor Crittenden to save Frank James from suffering the fate of his brother. On October 5, Edwards and Frank James walked into the office of the governor. "Governor Crittenden," Frank said, pulling out his revolvers, "I want to hand over to you that which no living man except myself has been permitted to touch since 1861, and to say that I am your prisoner."

The authorities charged Frank James with a number of the gang's crimes, from the murder of Captain Sheets at Gallatin to the Winston holdup. In a dramatic trial that featured the testimony of General Joseph Shelby himself, the jury acquitted Frank of all charges. He went on to live a quiet life with his family, farming and working a range of humble jobs.

The death of Jesse James proved a turning point for Governor Crittenden as well; it marked both the high point and the beginning of the end of his career. After his term ended in 1884, the Democrats turned away from this old Union man and elected former Confederate cavalry general John S. Marmaduke to take his place. The taint of the assassination of Jesse James prevented Crittenden from ever attaining high office again.

Over the last century, the legend of Jesse James has changed along with the country itself. From his origins on the tearing seam of the nation as it split into Civil War, through a guerrilla conflict as savage as any America has ever fought, to the vigilante rule and mob violence in the years that followed, Jesse James rose up in a land soaked in suspicion, hatred, and bloodshed. In this atmosphere, Major John Newman Edwards easily turned him into a local champion—vindicator of the genteel, chivalric, mythical South crushed by the Republican North. The spread of big business, especially the banks and railroads,

The body of Jesse James was photographed in its coffin by A. A. Hughes in 1882.

In this 1884 woodcut, a crowd celebrates Frank James's acquittal on all charges in Huntsville, Alabama. On October 5, 1882, Frank had turned himself in to stand trial. Surrendering his guns to Governor Crittenden, he said "I want to hand over to you that which no living man except myself has been permitted to touch since 1861, and to say that I am your prisoner."

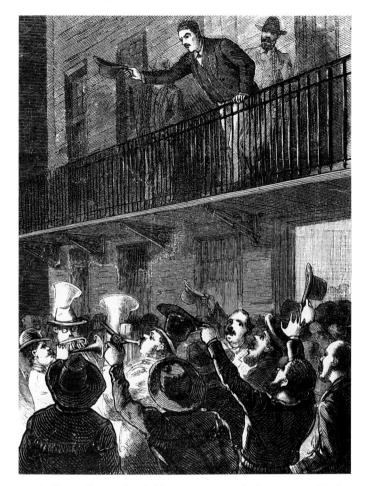

made Jesse James look like an economic hero as well, the avenger of the poor, independent small farmer.

But even before Jesse James's death, his legend began to change, and his fame as a national figure grew. To people in other states, unfamiliar with the vicious politics of Missouri, he looked like a hero of the Wild West rather than the Old South. As the 19th century rolled by, America changed with the spread of mass publications and the hucksterism of men like P. T. Barnum (who formed Barnum and Bailey's Circus in 1871). In these new, more commercial times, a minor industry rose up to capitalize on the widespread interest in Jesse James. Magazine

stories and paperback dime novels by the dozens fictionalized the adventures of the notorious James brothers.

Seemingly everyone involved in Jesse James's outlaw
career tried to cash in on his fame. Bob Ford made a career
out of promoting himself as "the man who shot Jesse
James," appearing in traveling Wild West shows, where he
reenacted the fatal shooting for paying audiences. He later
died at the hands of a little-known drifter named Ed Kelly,
who wanted to be known as "the man who shot the man
who shot Jesse James." Thomas Crittenden's son published the governor's memoirs, generously padding the
material with miscellaneous items about the James gang to
increase sales. Frank James, too, performed in Wild West
shows as he struggled to earn a living long after any
remaining loot had run out. Even Jesse James, Jr., the
outlaw's only son, once appeared in a silent movie, *Under*

*After his acquittal, Frank
James returned to a quiet life
with his family, farming and
working in other humble jobs.
The bookish Frank was never
as impulsive as his brother,
Jesse, especially after he
became weakened by a lung
disease that plagued him for
the latter half of his life.*

the Black Flag, as a publicity stunt. The appeal of the Jesse James saga has continued down to the present day, as a succession of adventure stories, movies, and television shows have fictionalized the historical character beyond all recognition.

Every September, more than a century after Jesse James's death, eight men ride rather average horses into Northfield, Minnesota, while an announcer introduces them to the crowds that line the streets. As a part of Northfield's annual outdoor festival, the "Defeat of Jesse James Days," several local actors reenact the climactic raid that failed in a storm of bullets in 1876. A shot-by-shot description blares over the loudspeaker as the actors gallop around, fire blanks in the air, and collapse to the ground, only to pick themselves up again at the end of the show. The announcer, of course, takes no time to describe the Civil War landscape of burning farms and mutilated dead, or the vigilantes and tax riots of Reconstruction, or the slow evolution of the wild Border region into a prosperous heartland. But the audience appreciates the action, and it loudly applauds the rousing performance before returning to carnival rides, shooting galleries, and cotton candy.

Zerelda Samuel stands in the yard of the old James homestead next to the grave of her son, Jesse James.

Further Reading

Baldwin, Margaret, and Pat O'Brien. *Wanted! Frank and Jesse James, the Real Story*. New York: Julian Messner, 1981.

Breihan, Carl W. *Saga of Jesse James*. Caldwell, ID: Caxton Printers, 1991.

Brown, Richard Maxwell. *No Duty To Retreat: Violence and Values in American History and Society*. New York: Oxford University Press, 1991.

Connelley, William E. *Quantrill and the Border Wars*. New York: Pageant, 1956.

Croy, Homer. *Jesse James Was My Neighbor*. New York: Duell, Sloan, and Pearce, 1949.

Fellman, Michael. *Inside War: The Guerrilla Conflict in Missouri During the American Civil War*. New York: Oxford University Press, 1986.

Freehling, William W. *The Road to Disunion, Volume I: Secessionists at Bay, 1776–1854*. New York: Oxford University Press, 1990.

Josephy, Alvin M., Jr. *The Civil War in the American West*. New York: Knopf, 1991.

McCorkle, John, with O. S. Barton. *Three Years with Quantrill*. Memphis: Lockhard, 1914.

McPherson, James M. *Battle Cry of Freedom: The Civil War Era*. New York: Oxford University Press, 1988.

McReynolds, Edwin C. *Missouri: A History of the Crossroads State*. Norman: University of Oklahoma Press, 1962.

Ross, James R. *I, Jesse James*. Los Angeles: Dragon, 1988.

Settle, William A., Jr. *Jesse James Was His Name*. Columbia: University of Missouri Press, 1966.

Thelen, David. *Paths of Resistance: Tradition and Dignity in Industrializing Missouri*. New York: Oxford University Press, 1986.

Chronology

September 5, 1847	Jesse Woodson James is born to the Reverend Robert and Zerelda James of Clay County, Missouri
1850	Robert James joins a gold rush expedition to California, where he dies
September 1855	Zerelda James marries Dr. Reuben Samuel
August 10, 1861	Frank James fights for the Confederacy in the Battle of Wilson's Creek as the Civil War erupts in Missouri
Summer 1863	Pro-Union militia men raid the Samuel farm, beating Jesse James and torturing his stepfather
Spring 1864	Jesse James joins "Bloody Bill" Anderson's guerrilla unit; loses a fingertip and suffers a severe chest wound that summer
Early 1865	The Samuel family is banished to Nebraska
May or June 1865	Jesse James rides to Lexington, Missouri, to surrender; is shot and badly wounded by Federal cavalrymen and makes his way to his family in Rulo, Nebraska
Summer 1865	Zerelda Samuel takes Jesse to Harlem, Missouri, where his cousin Zerelda "Zee" Mimms nurses him back to health; Jesse and Zee become engaged
February 13, 1866	A band of former guerrillas robs the Clay County Savings Bank in Liberty, Missouri
May 22, 1867	The same gang robs the bank in Richmond, Missouri; several of the bandits are lynched by mobs in the months that follow
December 7, 1869	Jesse and Frank James rob the Daviess County Savings Bank in Gallatin, Missouri, and murder Captain John W. Sheets
September 26, 1872	Jesse James and Cole and John Younger rob the Kansas City Fair; the next day Major John Newman Edwards publishes an editorial on the robbery, "The Chivalry of Crime," comparing the bandits to the Knights of the Round Table
July 21, 1873	The James-Younger gang robs its first train, the Chicago, Rock Island, and Pacific Railroad, at Council Bluffs, Iowa
March 1874	Jesse James and the Younger brothers kill three Pinkerton detectives; John Younger is shot dead
April 24, 1874	Jesse James marries Zee Mimms; they move to Texas briefly, then return to live in Kansas City, Missouri
January 26, 1875	The Pinkerton detectives bomb the Samuel home, killing Jesse James's half brother and maiming his mother

September 7, 1876	After a raid in Northfield, Minnesota, Cole, Bob, and Jim Younger are arrested; William Stiles, Clell Miller, and Samuel Wells are killed; and Jesse and Frank James are wounded but escape and move to Nashville, Tennessee
October 8, 1879	Jesse James returns to banditry when he robs a train at Glendale, Missouri, with a new gang that includes Bill Ryan
January 10, 1881	Thomas T. Crittenden is inaugurated as Missouri governor; William Wallace takes over as Jackson County prosecutor after denouncing the James brothers in his campaign
March 1881	Bill Ryan is arrested near Nashville and is taken back to Missouri to stand trial; Jesse James flees with his family to Kentucky, then Kansas City, and finally to St. Joseph, Missouri
July 15, 1881	Jesse and Frank James and their gang rob the Chicago, Rock Island, and Pacific Railroad at Winston, Missouri; Jesse kills conductor William Westfall
July 26, 1881	Governor Crittenden meets with the state's railroad executives in St. Louis; the railroads agree to provide reward money for the capture of the James brothers; two days later, the governor issues a proclamation offering $10,000 each for the arrest and conviction of Frank and Jesse James
September 1881	Bill Ryan stands trial and is convicted because of the testimony of Tucker Bassham, a former gang member; Bob Ford joins his brother Charlie as a member of Jesse James's gang
January 1882	Bob Ford meets with Governer Crittenden and agrees to assassinate Jesse James
April 4, 1882	Bob Ford shoots Jesse James in the back of the head while Jesse straightens a picture in his home

Index

T. J. Stiles is a free-lance writer living in the city of New York. He holds
advanced degrees in history from Columbia University in New York and a
bachelor's degree from Carleton College in Northfield, Minnesota (where he
regularly attended the annual Defeat of Jesse James Days). He is a native of
Minnesota, and according to family legend is related to William Stiles, the inept
member of the James gang who was killed in Northfield on September 7, 1876.

Vito Perrone is Director of Teacher Education and Chair of Teaching, Curriculum, and Learning Environments at Harvard University. He has previous
experience as a public school teacher, a university professor of history, education, and peace studies (University of North Dakota), and as dean of the New
School and the Center for Teaching and Learning (both at the University of
North Dakota). Dr. Perrone has written extensively about such issues as
educational equity, humanities curriculum, progressive education, and evalua-
tion. His most recent books are: *A Letter to Teachers: Reflections on Schooling
and the Art of Teaching*; *Enlarging Student Assessment in Schools*; *Working
Papers: Reflections on Teachers, Schools, and Communities*; *Visions of Peace*;
and *Johanna Knudsen Miller: A Pioneer Teacher.*